THE
AURA

THE
AURA

BY

WALTER J. KILNER, B.A., M.B. Cantab.,

M.R.C.P., ETC., LATE ELECTRICIAN AT
ST. THOMAS'S HOSPITAL, LONDON

Illustrated

INTRODUCTION BY
SIBYL FERGUSON

SAMUEL WEISER, INC.
York Beach, Maine

Originally published under the title
The Human Atmosphere in 1911
This American Paperback Edition, 1973
Seventh printing, 1984
Copyright © Samuel Weiser, Inc.

Published by
Samuel Weiser, Inc.
Box 612
York Beach, ME 03910

ISBN 0-87728-215-3
Library of Congress Catalog Card No. 72-92279

Printed in the United States by
Interstate Book Manufacturers, Inc.

FOREWORD

In 1869 Walter John Kilner joined the staff of London's St. Thomas' Hospital, where he served as physician and surgeon, and investigated electrotherapy.

This was an exciting, progressive period in medical history. Electrical treatment had been approved, and Professor W. K. Rontgen had introduced his great discovery—the Rontgen Rays or X-rays, as we say—to an incredulous world. By 1897 St. Thomas' Hospital established the first X-ray department in London, and Young Dr. Kilner was made the director of this new innovation.

Then, too, the medical and scientific worlds began to hear from outstanding men, discussing hitherto unorthodox subjects. Dr. H. Berheim and Dr. James Braid wrote learnedly on hypnosis. The famous German scientist, Baron Carl von Reichenbach, published his findings on what he termed the "Odic force," that luminous emanation surrounding the body. In America Dr. Edwin Babbitt spoke highly of von Reichenbach. He then continued with what became a monumental study of color and healing. In his book, *The Principles of Light and Color,* he discusses how the life forces are revealed through methods he describes.

The work of these men had not escaped Dr. Kilner. Also, he was aware of the claims of clairvoyants, who described the light surrounding the human, which they interpreted as indications of character and health. He had seen the Theosophical writings of Leadbeater on the aura, which had been illustrated with paintings of the emanations. Furthermore there were many famous paintings depicting the nimbus above the heads of the saints and other holy people.

Kilner's active, scientific mind analyzed all his findings, both physical and occult. He accepted the presence of the aura, and he determined to make it visible to the human eye. Working with a coaltar dye, known as dicyanin, he was finally rewarded. The effect of dicyanin upon the sight of the eye is very marked. Looking through a lens painted with the chemical substance, the eye is enabled to perceive into the ultra-violet range.

Within this range the aura is seen as an inner band outlining the body, while a second band of almost vaporous light extends outward.

By sensitizing the eyes with the Kilner Screen (literally lenses coated with dicyanin) the aura may be seen as a gray-blue emanation, which is an aid to diagnosing disease. The condition of the aura reveals the states of health or illness. This was not a secret process, but one available to all who cared to use it.

When Dr. Kilner published his book, *The Human Atmosphere* (now being published under the title *The Aura*), it was not well received. ''The British Medical Journal'' in the January 6, 1912 issue said,

"Dr. Kilner has failed to convince us that his aura is more real than Macbeth's visionary dagger." In today's language he was definitely "ahead of his time." Although he had emphatically stated from the beginning that his work was completely divorced from the occult, his research was professionally discredited.

Because Dr. Kilner was a man of determination and conviction, he continued with his experiments, until World War One cut off his supply of dicyanin, which had been produced in Germany.

He resigned his position at St. Thomas' and discontinued his practice, retiring to Bury St. Edmund to assist his brother Charles, a well-known physician with a very large practice.

In 1920 a revised edition of Kilner's book was published. Early in 1921 a favorable book review appeared in the "Medical Times." Now recognized medical men endorsed his work. But it was too late, for Dr. Kilner had died in June of 1920.

It has been said that Dr. Kilner's sons who followed their father in becoming physicians, did not pursue his study of the aura.

The one outstanding scientific man to investigate the aura is Oscar Bagnall. As a young man he knew Dr. Kilner and benefited through his knowledge. Bagnall, too, wrote a book on the subject, *The Origin and Properties of the Human Aura,* which is vindication of Dr. Kilner's claims.

Incongruously, it was the very people whom Dr. Kilner, the scientific researcher, emphatically thrust aside who have kept his name and work alive. The clairvoyants, the metaphysicians and occultists claimed him as their own, even though their interpretation differed. Dr. Kilner knew the aura to be purely physical, while the followers believed it was of the Spirit.

Today in medical laboratories scientific experimentation regarding the aura is being attempted. It has been claimed that the emanations surrounding the body have been measured and photographed by serious, practical men. This is the age of acceptance and willing research into the less known. So the reissue of Dr. Kilner's book is coming at the appropriate time.

NEW YORK

Sibyl Ferguson

PREFACE

The perception of the Human Atmosphere or Aura, by the sole employment of material means, at once makes the phenomenon a physical question. From the first moment of seeing the human atmosphere, I determined to investigate the subject apart from all occultism; and, to remain unbiased, did not read any accounts of the Aura until a large number (over sixty) of patients had been inspected. As all the descriptions and references to the Aura that could be found were, without exception, in occult works, and afforded little assistance to physical investigation, I have decided to insert no quotations. This resolution places me in a peculiar position of having no authorities to fall back upon, which in some ways is an advantage, and a disadvantage in others.

The title of Human Atmosphere—a happy inspiration of a friend—is especially appropriate to the subject, because it conveys a clear idea to the general public, while the term "Aura," notwithstanding its definition—"any subtle, invisible emanation, effluvium, or exhalation from a substance, as aroma of flowers, etc." (Webster's Dictionary)—is confined to people possessing some knowledge of occultism. The word Aura has, however, been retained for shortness and convenience, as "Atmosphere" would be misleading when used alone, and when combined with "Human" is, to say the least, cumbersome.

After what has been said about the desire to be perfectly free from Occultism, it may seem strange that the expression Etheric Double has been employed. This name was borrowed from theosophic books, as no appropriate term has as yet been devised.

W. J. K.

218 LADBROKE GROVE,
  LONDON.

TABLE OF CONTENTS

CHAPTER VI

CHAPTER VII

LIST OF ILLUSTRATIONS

TABLES AND CASES

TABLES

CASES

THE HUMAN ATMOSPHERE

OR

THE AURA MADE VISIBLE BY THE AID OF CHEMICAL SCREENS

CHAPTER I

THE AURA OF HEALTHY PERSONS

HARDLY one person in ten thousand is aware that he or she is surrounded by a haze intimately connected with the body, whether asleep or awake, whether hot or cold, which, although invisible under ordinary circumstances, can be seen when conditions are favourable. This mist, the prototype of the halo or nimbus constantly depicted around the saints, has been manifested to certain individuals possessing a specially gifted sight, who have received the title of "Clairvoyants," and until quite recently, to no one else. The cloud or atmosphere, or, as it is generally termed, Aura, is the

1

subject of this treatise, in so far as it can be perceived by the employment of screens containing a peculiar chemical substance in solution. It may as well be stated at once that we make not the slightest claim to clairvoyancy; nor are we occultists; and we especially desire to impress on our readers that our researches have been entirely physical, and can be repeated by any one who takes sufficient interest in the subject.

As long as the faculty of perceiving the Aura is confined to a few individuals, and ordinary people have no means of corroboration or refutation, the door to imposture is open. Since this has been the case up to the present time, the subject has always been looked on askance; but there is no more charlatanism in the detection of the human Aura by the methods we employ, than in distinguishing microbes by the aid of the microscope. The main difference lies in the claim of some people that they are able to perceive the one through the possession of abnormal eyesight, while no one has had the hardihood to assert that they had the power of seeing an object one-thousandth of a millimeter in length without instrumental aid. There cannot be the smallest doubt as to the reality of the existence of an Aura enveloping human beings, and this will be in a short time an universally accepted fact, now that it can be made visible to any one possessing normal eyesight. It would, indeed, be strange if the Aura did not vary under different circumstances, and we firmly believe that a study of its modifications will show that they will have a diagnostic value.

We must ask the indulgence of our readers while we make a few personal remarks. Every thing that has been stated in this book as being a fact, is true; but we know that enthusiasm and imagination are wont to lead experimenters astray, and we have consequently endeavoured to do our best not to overstate any incident. This in one part of our subject is most difficult, because so much depends on subjective vision. It is only fair to add, however, that sight is our most perfect sense; and, consequently, we may perhaps have been able to distinguish objects a little in excess of the average, and may thus have perceived effects which might have es-

caped the notice of other observers. Some of
the deductions may be thought, and perhaps
rightly, to be too dogmatic, since they are
founded upon such a small number of cases;
but our excuse is that they have been brought
forward with the intention of their being working hypotheses to assist in future observations.
The discovery of a *screen* capable of making
the Aura visible was by no means accidental.
After reading about the actions of the "N"
Rays upon phosphorescent sulphide of calcium,
we were for some time experimenting on the
mechanical force of certain emanations from
the body, and had come to the conclusion,
whether rightly or wrongly, that we had detected two forces besides heat that could act
upon our needles, and that these forces were
situated in the ultra red portion of the spectrum.

There was a hitch in our experiments; and,
in the early part of 1908, we thought that certain dyes might assist us. After considering
the different spectra and, as far as we could,
ascertaining their properties, we made trial of
several, and fixed upon one which in this trea-

tise will be called *Spectauranine*[1] as the most likely to be of use. As we were compelled to wait some time before we were able to obtain it, one night the thought flashed across us that that substance might make some portion of the above mentioned forces visible; and, if so, we expected it would be the human Aura. This phenomenon we had heard about, but until that moment we had never had any intention of investigating it, as we believed it to be beyond our natural powers.

As soon as the chemical had been received, screens made of glass coated with collodion, and also gelatine dyed with it, were made, but were found to be entirely useless owing to decomposition taking place immediately. Afterwards

---

[1] Some friends, who have carefully considered the question, recommend the real name of the dye employed to be divulged. This we are quite willing to do, only it is too late to alter the term "Spectauranine" throughout the text, as the book is in the hands of the printers. The real name of the dye is "*Dicyanin.*" The blue screens accompanying the book merely contain a solution of dicyanin, and the red contain carmine. These four screens are the only ones necessary for ordinary observations of the Aura.

There is evidently a great difficulty in the manufacture of these thin flat cells, as we could find no one in Great Britain or in America who would undertake to make them, but at last we have succeeded in finding a foreign firm able to construct them.

a celluloid solution called *Zapon* was tried. This gave a better result; but, in a few hours' time, it, too, lost its colour. Subsequently solutions in alcohol of different strengths in glass cells were employed. These seem on the whole to be satisfactory, but there is tendency after a time for colour changes to take place, even if kept in the dark as much as possible. As a rule only two screens are necessary: one containing a solution of spectauranine in alcohol, and a second less dilute. Others of various strengths, with and without the addition of other dyes, have been tried, but these were only for purposes of experiment under differing circumstances. For ordinary work these are unnecessary. However, another kind of screen will be found useful for differentiating the separate parts of the Aura, which will be described later on.

Directly a screen was finished, we looked at a friend through it, and instantly saw around his head and hands a faint greyish cloud, which we considered could be nothing else but the Aura. After a few minutes we were surprised to find that we could continue to see the Aura without the intervention of the screen. This power did not last long. However, it was renewed by looking at the light for a few seconds through a dark screen.

It is interesting to note that this capacity for seeing the Aura without the intervention of the screen is by no means uncommon, but generally exists only for a short while. At this period every spare moment was occupied in using the screen for this and other experiments in connection with the perception of the Aura, consequently we discovered to our cost that the spectauranine had a very deleterious effect upon our eyes, making them very painful, so much so that it was necessary to cease work for some days. On account of this, we strongly recommend all experimenters on this subject, not to be continually looking through the spectauranine screen. Apparently the action of this chemical is cumulative, so that we gradually gained the power of seeing the Aura more and more plainly without the intervention of the screen. Ultimately our eyes have become so permanently affected that under suitable conditions we are able to dispense with a screen.

Nevertheless, we think it expedient to look at the light for a few seconds through a spectauranine screen before inspection, and even then we sometimes find the Aura is better seen through a light one. At other times the reverse holds good, though the conditions may be exactly similar in the two cases.

The Aura can only be satisfactorily defined when certain conditions are fulfilled. The light must not be too bright. The requisite amount must be determined at each observation, and depends on whether a screen is being used or not. A rough estimate is, that the body can just be seen distinctly after the observer has become accustomed to the dulness. The light ought to be diffused, coming from one direction only, and falling on the patient equally all over. Certainly, the best arrangement is obtained when the observer is standing with his back to a darkened window while the patient faces it. An alternative method, if the room is sufficiently large and open, and the only one that can be employed at a patient's house, is to have a tent similar to the X folding portable dark-room as used for photography, except that it must be lined with black instead of the ordinary yellow material, and the front curtains must be removed. The tent is placed with its back to the window and the patient stands inside, when he will be evenly illuminated. All the windows in the room, except the one at the back of the tent, should be completely darkened, while this one must have the blind drawn more or less as required. The chief objection to this arrangement is, that the observer has to stand facing the light, which is not so comfortable for any part of the inspection, and is especially inconvenient for the observations connected with the complementary colours, as will be described later on. Occasionally it is possible at a patient's house, with a little manœvering, to be able to place the tent with its opening facing the window. When this is done inspection is rendered much easier. It is essential to have the black background as dead black as is obtainable.

Most of our investigations have been conducted in a small room with only one window. This window is fitted at the top with an ordinary blind, and from below a blind of black serge can be raised to any height required. The serge allows a considerable amount of light to pass through, in fact too much, except on very dark days; but the amount can be regulated by pulling down the ordinary blind. This arrangement is also very convenient, as a slight gap can be left between the two blinds so as to allow much more light into the room when the patient is being observed through the dark carmine screen, and also occasionally when the complementary colours are employed.

Opposite, and about eight feet from the window is a movable pole supporting black and white curtains, either of which can be used as wanted. The white background is necessary for certain observations, which will be described farther on. These are all the arrangements that are required.

There is one point that is important to bear in mind, namely, that the patient should stand about a foot in front of the background, so that shadows or marks upon it may not produce any optical illusions, and thus vitiate the observations. Trouble of this kind is not likely to occur, except when the observer is new to the work.

While the patient is assuming the proper position, the observer takes the dark screen and peers through it at the light for half a minute or longer. This will influence his eyesight for a sufficiently long time, so that it will rarely be necessary to repeat the operation. However, repetition can be made as often as desired. He now darkens the room and regulates the light; and, standing with his back to the window and opposite the patient, looks at him through a pale screen, when he ought to perceive immediately or (if not accustomed to the work) after a few seconds a faint cloud enveloping the patient, which varies in health according to individual peculiarities. If the observer has already gained the ability of perceiving the Aura without the intervention of the screen, he will usually find it to have some shade of blue. It is certainly of assistance in determining the colour of the Aura, if the patient places his hands upon his hips and at the same time extends his elbows, when, in the spaces between the trunk and the arms, the Aura emanating from the body will be reinforced by that proceeding from the arms.

When commencing a systematic inspection it will be advisable for the patient first to face the observer and the light. The Aura round the head will be best seen while he stands or sits with his hands hanging by his sides. Its breadth may roughly be determined by noticing how far it extends beyond the shoulders, and this permits the two sides to be compared, because in some cases of disease the Aura will be wider or narrower on one side than on the other. At this stage attention ought to be paid to the general shape of the Aura while the arms are hanging down, as this often differs greatly from that seen when they are uplifted. For the greater part of the inspection it will be found advantageous for the patient to stand with his hands behind his neck, so that the Aura from the axilla down the trunk, thighs, and legs may be seen uninfluenced by the Aura proceeding from the arms. This is the time to determine the shape and size of the Aura, whether it follows the contour of the body or whether it is wider by the trunk than the lower limbs; and, if so, how far it descends before it finally narrows.   It is not uncommon for some abnormality of texture to be visible, but this, as a rule, can be differentiated with greater accuracy by the employment of special screens.

Occasionally the Aura can be separated by its appearance into two or, very rarely, three distinct portions, but the verification of this division will be better made at a later stage of the examination.   As soon as all the information as to the Aura at the sides has been gained, the patient must be turned sideways, so that the Aura at the front and back may be similarly examined.   If any suspicion should arise as to the Aura being unequally illuminated, it must be (in addition to the foregoing inspection), viewed when the back is turned to the light, and again when turned sideways in the direction opposite to the one he previously assumed.   By this simple means a number of errors are eliminated.   The Aura envelops the whole of the human frame, but, on account of the fineness of its texture and its transparency, it is only visible in sections; consequently when the observer wishes to examine the Aura emanating from one particular spot, he will be obliged to turn the patient to a different angle, so that a silhouette of this spot may be made on the background. Generally, if the shape of the Aura is the only thing required, it can be ascertained by the patient first standing facing the observer, and then sideways without any other movement. Considerations of the other portions of the systematic inspection must be deferred for the present.

Examination of a number of people in good health shows not merely, as might be expected, individual differences, but also the existence of a corporate dissimilarity. Males, independent of age, possess the same characteristics of the Aura, after making allowance for individual peculiarities, as no two people are alike. Quite the opposite is the case in females, because their Auras undergo a great alteration of shape at certain periods of their lives. In childhood it coincides almost exactly with that of the male. In adults it is much more developed, while in adolescence—from twelve to thirteen until eighteen to twenty years—it slowly advances from the masculine type to that of adult womanhood.

Inspection of a man discloses the Aura enveloping the head fairly equally all round, it being about two inches broader than the width of the shoulders. When he stands facing the observer, with his arms raised and his hands at the back of his neck, the Aura will appear by the side of his trunk narrower than round his head, following closely the contour of the body. Here it does not usually exceed more than four or five inches in width, or, roughly speaking, one-fifteenth of his height. As soon as he has turned sideways, it will be seen down his back about as broad as by the sides of the trunk, but barely as wide as in front. In all these cases it is similarly continued down the lower limbs, only sometimes being a little narrower. Around the arms it corresponds with that encircling the legs, but is generally broader around the hands, and very frequently it projects a long distance from the tips of the fingers.

Before a girl has arrived at the age of twelve or thirteen the description of the Aura of the males will be equally applicable to her. Nevertheless, the texture of the Aura is usually finer than that of a man, so that it occasionally becomes difficult to distinguish the edge of the haze. In like manner, but not to the same extent, the Auras of young boys may be faint. This prevents children from being good subjects for early observations. On observing the Aura of an adult woman a characteristic alteration is found. Above the shoulders round the head, down the arms and hands it is very similar to that of the males. If she faces the observer with the hands placed behind the neck, the dissimilarity is at once noticeable. The Aura is much wider by the sides of the trunk than in men, and broadens out until, at the level of the waist, it has reached its full extent. From here downwards, it gradually narrows until it reaches a point not higher than the middle of the thigh, where it finally contracts and follows the outline of the legs and feet. However, the point of final contraction may be anywhere between the place just mentioned and the ankles.

As she stands sideways, the Aura will be seen to be much wider at the back than at the front, and the broadest part is at the small of the back where it frequently bulges out. From thence it comes down from near the nates, following the contour of the legs and thighs. In front it takes the outline of the body, being a little wider at the chest and abdomen than lower down. It is not uncommon to find the haze more pronounced in front of the breasts and nipples, and this increase is evidently dependent upon the functional activity of the glands, as it is most apparent during pregnancy and lactation, but is occasionally the same just before or after menstruation. When the Aura is fully developed age does not produce any alteration, but disease may. Figs. 9 to 13 are good specimens of the Aura of a woman in health.

Amongst healthy women the Aura shows many departures from the above examples. The modifications consist in the difference of width by the side of the trunk and the distance it descends, before it has contracted to its fullest extent, and follows the contour of the body. Besides, it will be noticed that the breadth in front of the body often alters, but not nearly to the same extent. At the back, changes are more frequent and varied. These are chiefly due to differences in breadth and the position of the final contraction. With one person the outer margin of the haze is apparently quite straight from the level of the shoulders to the most prominent part of the nates, and from thence it follows the outline of the body downwards. With another person it will bulge out at the small of the back, contracting when it reaches the middle of the thigh, or it may be near the ground before it follows the figure. Occasionally the Aura proceeds downwards from over the head to the feet without coming near the body. This we consider to be the most perfect shape. Any deviations are due to undevelopment. The average width of the Aura over a woman round the waist is eight to ten inches, and on some not more than six or seven inches, but it may reach twelve or more (*vide* Figs. 9, 11, 13).

When a girl approaches the age of puberty her Aura begins to show an alteration, leaving the infantile form to attain, in from four to six years, the shape assumed by an adult woman. The change does not usually commence until a short time before menstruation appears, but

never before the body has begun to develop.
Exceptions to this are occasionally met with.
For instance, a girl fourteen years old (Case 9,
Figs. 7 and 8) had a marked Transitional Aura,
but did not menstruate for six months after.
The youngest child who showed any increase
of Aura was thirteen and a half years old.
She was a remarkably well developed child
for her age, but suffered from epileptic fits; six
months previously she had an infantile Aura.
Three others of fourteen, one of fifteen, four of
sixteen, one of seventeen, and one of nineteen
years of age, possessed Auras in a transitional
state, while two others of eighteen years of age
had fully formed Auras. One undersized,
weakly girl, nearly seventeen years old, who had
never menstruated, retained a perfectly infantile shape of Aura, which, however, was well
marked. On the other hand, a tall, well-formed
young woman, twenty-five years of age, who had
an undeveloped uterus, and who had only menstruated four times in her life (the last period
being three years ago), is the possessor of a very
distinct Aura, much larger than the average.
Another woman, forty-two years of age, who

had both her ovaries removed sixteen years ago, had a fairly marked Aura quite up to the average in width by the sides of the trunk, but especially broad at the back and front.

There can be no two opinions as to the enlargement of the female Aura at the period of adolescence, but it remains to be proved whether this is entirely due to the functional maturity of the sexual organs, or whether the other changes which have taken place in the system contribute to its development. But this much can be confidently stated, as will appear later on, that menstruation has a subtle effect on the Aura, while the changes in shape in early pregnancy are not very pronounced. During a later period a great extension in front of the breast and the lower part of the abdomen may appear, but this is only temporary and local. The subject will be discussed later on.

For the sake of simplicity, and to avoid unnecessary repetition in the above description, the Aura has been treated as if it were a simple phenomenon, while in reality it is composite.

Later on its elements will be fully considered, but for the present it will be sufficient to say that it can be divided into three parts.

First, there is a narrow transparent portion appearing as a dark space, which is very often obliterated by the second portion of the Aura. When visible it looks like a dark band, not exceeding a quarter of an inch, surrounding and adjacent to the body, without any alteration in size at any part. This will be called the *Etheric Double*.

The second constituent is the *Inner Aura*. It is the densest portion and varies comparatively little, or even not at all, in width, either at the back, front, or sides, and both in the male and the female follows the contour of the body. It arises just outside the Etheric Double, but very frequently it looks as if it touched the body itself.

The third portion, or the *Outer Aura*, commences at the outer edge of the Inner Aura, and is very variable in size. It is the extreme outer margin of this that has been taken for depicting the outline of the Aura hitherto. When the whole Aura is observed through a light spectauranine screen, or a pale blue one, all the portions appear blended together, but the part nearest the body is the most dense. If, however, a carmine screen be employed, each of the factors will be distinguished; or, should this screen be a fairly dark one, the Outer Aura will be eliminated altogether.

The following descriptions of the Auras are from a selection of persons in good health, varying in age from early infancy and upwards, and are typical. They are arranged according to age—first males, and then females.

CASE 1.—A., a fine, healthy infant, fifteen hours old, was inspected whilst lying on its mother's bed upon a black cloth. Although seen under very unfavourable circumstances, his Aura was plainly visible, and in colour was grey, tinged with yellow. As far as could be seen it followed the outline of the body. This is the youngest child whose Aura we have examined, and it may be interesting to note that both the mother and the nurse were able to see the cloud around him, if they looked through the screen.

When he had arrived at the age of four months, he was inspected again under more

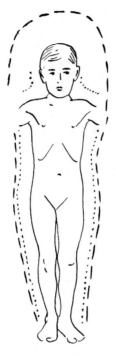

FIG. 1.—Healthy boy.

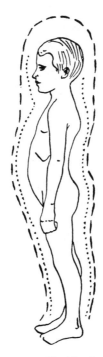

Fig. 2.—Healthy boy.

suitable conditions, being then placed on a sofa, with a black cloth under him. His Aura took the same outline as the body, being a little over an inch wide, with the exception of the part round the head, which was broader. The colour had changed to dark blue grey.

CASE 2. — B., when a healthy male infant of four months old, was examined while lying on a black cloth similar to the background behind him; his Aura could be easily detected, being of a bluish grey colour. The Outer Aura was seen about an inch wide around his body and limbs, but by the sides of the head it was a little broader than the width of the shoulders.

When examined through a dark carmine screen, the Inner Aura was quite distinct, about three-quarters of an inch wide, showing well-marked striation.

CASE 3 (Figs. 1 and 2). — C., a strong and healthy lad, five years old, who had never had any serious illness. While he stood facing the observer, his Outer Aura appeared to be about six inches round the head. It came down by the side of the trunk about three and a quarter inches, and was a little narrower by the lower part of the thighs and the legs. The Inner Aura could be plainly distinguished, being nearly two inches wide by the side of the head and trunk, and about one and a quarter by the legs. When he turned sideways, the Outer Aura was found to be about two inches wide in front, and the Inner about a quarter of an inch less.

Both these measurements were slightly diminished lower down. At the back the Outer Aura was two and a half inches wide by the trunk, but not quite so wide by the lower limbs. Here, too, the Inner was about a quarter of an inch less than the Outer Aura. The colour was a blue grey. It is worthy of notice that in children, especially among males, the Inner Aura is almost as wide as the Outer; and often the two can only be differentiated with difficulty.

CASE 4.—D., a youth, fourteen years old. He is rather tall for his age, and has enjoyed good health all his life. His Aura was well marked, and a bluish grey. As he stood facing the observer, the Outer Aura was seven inches

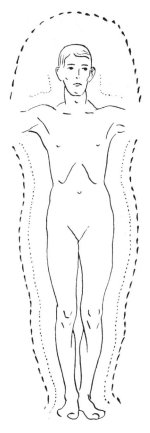

Fig. 3.—Healthy, very strong man.

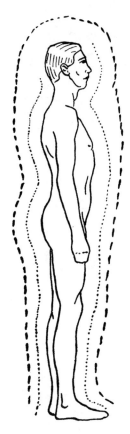

Fig. 4.—Healthy, very strong man.

round his head, by the side of his trunk four inches, and lower down three and a half inches. The Inner Aura was two inches wide all over the body.

The Etheric Double was visible, being one-eighth of an inch wide. When he stood sideways, the Outer Aura was about three inches wide by his shoulders and nates, consequently for a male was rather wide at the small of the back. In front the Aura was three inches wide down the whole length.

CASE 5 (Figs. 3 and 4).—E., a very powerful man, thirty-three years of age. He was well proportioned in every respect, and in robust health. His Aura was blue with a little grey. The Outer Aura surrounded his head a little wider than the breadth of his shoulders; all down his trunk, arms, and legs it was five inches wide. The Inner Aura was extremely well marked, about three inches wide. Striation was remarkably easy to see. As he stood sideways, the Inner Aura was the same width both front and back, but the Outer was a trifle narrower in front. The Etheric Double was clearly defined, being nearly a quarter of an inch wider. His whole Aura was unusually coarse in texture.

CASE 6.—F., a female child, a week old, was inspected while she lay upon her mother's bed on a black cloth. The external conditions were extremely unfavourable, but, with a little difficulty, the Aura was seen as a greenish haze which followed the outline of the body, being very narrow; but around the head it increased a little, as might be expected.

When this infant had arrived at the age of four months (corresponding with that of A), she was examined a second time under better conditions. The Aura was very difficult to perceive, as it was not nearly as distinct as expected, and was only half an inch wide round her body, and rather broader round the head. The most interesting point was that the colour had changed from greenish to a gray shade.

CASE 7.—G., a fragile, excitable child, four years old, rather small for her age but in good health, was observed in January, 1910. She had a very extensive Aura for her age and size. The Outer was three inches wide all over her body, except round her head, where it extended to

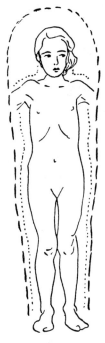

FIG. 5.—Healthy young girl.

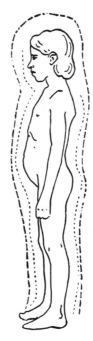

FIG. 6.—Healthy young girl.

nearly five inches. The inner was also distinct, striated, and two and a half inches wide. The colour was blue.

CASE 8 (Figs. 5 and 6).—H., a strong, healthy girl, seven years of age, who had never had any illness. The colour of her Aura was blue. As she stood facing the observer, the Outer Aura was half a foot round her head. By the side of her trunk it was three inches, gradually narrowing to two by her lower limbs. As she stood sideways, her Outer Aura measured two inches down the front, and three at the widest part of the back, and lower down it was two inches in width. The Inner Aura was two inches round her head and trunk, elsewhere only one and a half inches. She showed no rays.

CASE 9 (Figs. 7 and 8).—I. This example is extremely interesting, as we have been allowed to inspect her from time to time, and thus able to follow the growth of her Aura at the different periods of her early adolescence. She is a girl thirteen years of age, in good health. She has lately been developing fast, but has not yet menstruated. In October, 1908, she was inspected, when her Aura was found to be the same as in most young girls, following the outlines of the body, being about two inches wide, except around the head, where it was wider. The colour was blue.

After the lapse of eight months she had the appearance of that of a small, well-shaped, full-grown woman, but she had not as yet menstruated. Her Aura had now entered into the transitional state. Around the head it was a little broader than at her shoulders; by the side of her trunk it was about four inches wide, and about two and a half by her thighs and legs. When she turned sideways, the Aura showed an increase to two and a half at the small of the back, but in front was not more than two inches wide.

March, 1910. She has grown a little and is a shapely girl, being just fourteen and a half years old, and is in good health. Her first period came just a month ago. The Aura has enlarged. It is now five and a half inches by the side of and over the head. As she stands facing the observer, along the trunk it is four and a half in width, contracting further down to

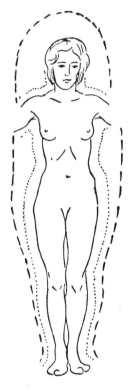

Fig. 7.—Healthy girl (Transitional Aura).

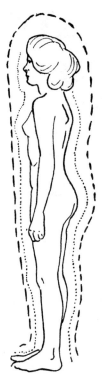

Fig. 8.—Healthy girl (Transitional Aura).

two and a half inches. When she turns sideways, in front it is seen to be three inches, while
at the back, at the widest part, it is four, and
gradually lower down it lessens to two and a
half inches. The Inner Aura is two inches wide
all over the body. It is easily perceived and
plainly striated. The Etheric Double could
just be discerned. Four months later the Aura
had increased by the side of the trunk by a good
half inch, but elsewhere it remained unaltered
in measurement.

This case is instructive, as the girl retained
her juvenile Aura quite six months after she
had commenced her outward bodily development, and the Aura in its turn began to evolve
twelve months before she first menstruated. It
is also a good example of the slowness with
which the Aura changes from the infantile to
the adult type.

CASE 10 (Figs. 9 and 10).—K., aged twenty-
six years, the mother of B. Her Aura was
what might be expected in a perfectly average
woman of her age. When she stood facing the
observer, the Outer Aura measured eight
inches round the head, and when she upraised
her arms, it was the same by her trunk. From

here it decreased until it had arrived at the lower part of the thighs, where it was three inches wide, and continued the same downwards. The Inner Aura measured two and a half inches all over the body. It was well marked, and striation could be easily detected. By the right side of the head the Aura was brighter and looked as if it were a broad, faint ray. It reached the whole width of the shoulders, and proceeded upwards as high as the level of the crown of the head. When she turned sideways, the Outer Aura in front was three inches broad, while at the back it was four at the widest part. The C. C. band was even all over the body, but the left extension was a little lighter than the right. The colour of the Aura was grey, with a slight blue shade.

CASE 11 (Figs. 11 and 12).—L., a fine, well-built woman, thirty years of age, who has always been strong and healthy. She has naturally a very even temper. Her Aura is blue, and is one of the finest we have seen, being, as she faces the observer, *egg-shaped.* The Outer Aura is quite twelve inches round the head and body, gradually contracting to about five inches at the ankles. The absolute edge

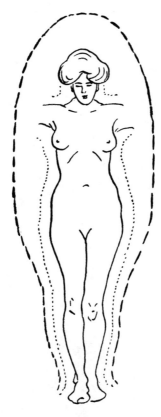

FIG. 9.—Healthy woman (Average Aura).

FIG. 10.—Healthy woman (Average Aura).

is difficult to define, but gives the impression of some imperceptible haze beyond, which observation we do not think is an optical illusion, as we have noticed it in other cases. This we have termed the *Ultra Outer Aura* (see page 82). As she stands sideways, the Outer Aura in front is five inches wide all the way down. At the back it is five inches at the shoulders, widening to eight in the lumbar regions, and contracting again to about four inches at the ankles. The Inner Aura is even all over the body, being three inches wide. The Etheric Double is nearly a quarter of an inch wide.

CASE 12 (Fig. 13).—M., a married woman, twenty-five years of age. In shape her Aura was quite ordinary for a woman of her years. She had, however, two rays running upwards and outwards from each shoulder. Another one on the left side also proceeded from near the axilla, and came downwards. The colour of her Aura was grey-blue. There was also a small ray emitted from a small fibro-adenoid tumour. The Inner Aura was three inches wide all over.

As heredity plays such an important part

in determining the qualities of so many constituents of the human body, it would be exceedingly strange if peculiarities of the Aura were not transmitted by descent. This part of the subject will, of course, require long and numerous observations before the question can be settled definitely, but even the few cases of two or more individuals in the same family, which have already been examined, show that this surmise is most likely correct. It is fairly easy to compare the Auras of adults one with another when they are all of one sex. But difficulties commence when the comparison has to be made between a man and a woman, since the masculine Aura is so very dissimilar from the feminine; and, for the same reason, comparison between a woman's Aura and a child's is difficult. Practically the only method is to compare the breadth of the Aura of the trunk of the subjects, as they stand facing the observer.

For this purpose some standard will be requisite. One thing is patent—that is, the height of a patient does not make very much difference in the breadth of the Aura, since a tall man or woman does not seem to have his or her Aura

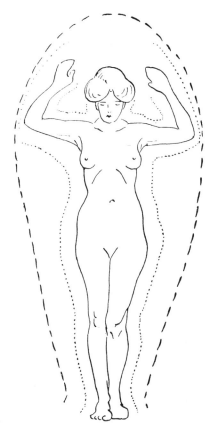

Fig. 11.—Healthy woman (very fine Aura).

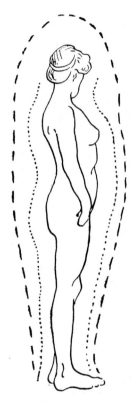

Fig. 12.—Healthy woman (very fine Aura).

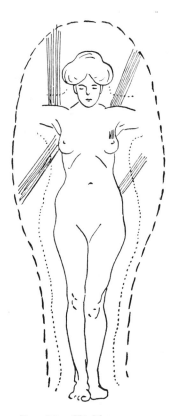

Fig. 13.—Healthy woman.

much, if any, wider than a short person, thus
destroying any chance of finding a working
ratio between the height of the subject and the
breadth of the Aura.   Besides, it must be remembered that children have relatively broader
Auras in proportion to their height than adults.
To add to the difficulty, abnormalities have to
be taken into consideration, although in these
instances one may find similar deviations in
other members of the family.

Since the ratio between the height of the
patient and the breadth of the Aura is pre-
cluded, there seems to be only one way of ob-
taining the required standard available, and
that is not a very satisfactory one.   This is to
fix, arbitrarily, the limits of the average dimensions of the Aura, and to take any deviations
from it as abnormal.   Taking this as a principle, all Auras may be divided into three divisions, viz.: wide, average, or narrow.   Roughly,
the Auras of women may be called "average,"
when they are from eight to ten inches broad
by the side of the trunk, in their widest part.

The standard for men may be taken as from
three and a half to four and a half inches, and

for children between two and a half to three inches. As the Auras of adolescent girls are changing from month to month, they will have to be considered each upon its own merits, as no hard and fast rule can be made. These figures have been decided on by experience only, and not by any scientific plan. Although this arrangement seems very simple, yet it is by no means always easy to decide whether a case is to be termed average or not.

Taking one instance alone: suppose a woman had an Aura, by the side of the trunk a little larger than the limits laid down for the average width, and this contracted down the thighs and legs (in fact, being the hysterical type of Aura) to below the average, under what heading should it be placed? This case, too, must be considered on its own merits. The following tables contain all the examples which have been investigated of two or more individuals of the same family up to date. The first table contains those cases where two[1] generations are involved, and the second belongs to the same generation. In two instances the same person comes into both tables.

---

[1] And in one family three.

TABLE I.—PARENTS AND CHILDREN

Name.	Sex.	Age.	Wide.	Aver-age.	Nar-row.	Condition.
N.	F.	25	W.	....	....	Healthy
Child	M.	4 months	W.	....	....	Healthy
U.	F.	30	W.	....	....	Healthy—Case 2
L. U.	M.	3½	W.	....	....	Healthy
H.	F.	24	....	....	N.	Healthy—Case 6
Child	F.	4 months	....	....	N.	Healthy
D.	F.	28	....	A.	....	Healthy
C. D.	M.	3½	....	A.	....	Healthy
M.	F.	38	....	A.	....	Healthy
K. M.	M.	5	....	A.	....	Healthy
M. M.	F.	7	....	A.	....	Healthy—Case 26
I. X.	M.	58	....	....	N.	Neurotic—Case 18
X. X.	M.	23	....	....	N.	Epileptic—Case 15
B. X.	F.	19	....	....	N.	Epileptic—Case 16
C.	F.	29	....	....	N.	Married daughter, healthy
F. X.	F.	12½	....	....	N.	Granddaughter, dull
G. X.	F.	9½	....	A.	....	Granddaughter
E. X.	F.	7¾	W.	....	....	Hysterical—Case 14
C. C.	M.	59	....	....	N.	Chronic Bright's disease
D. C.	F.	23	....	....	N.	Hysterical
C. C. C.	F.	36	....	A.	....	Healthy
F. C.	F.	10	....	A.	....	Healthy
C. C. C. C.	F.	39	....	A.	....	Healthy
S. C.	F.	6	....	A.	....	Healthy
N. N.	F.	33	....	A.[1]	....	Hysterical Aura
R. N.	F.	6	....	A.	....	Healthy
O.	F.	63	....	A.	....	Hemiplegic
O. O.	F.	28	....	A.	....	Hysterical
G.	F.	26	....	A.	....	Healthy—Case 10
Child	M.	4 months	....	A.	....	Healthy

[1] It would have been considered wide except that it was narrow by the thighs and legs. Her daughter's Aura is on the border of being wide.

TABLE II.—BROTHERS AND SISTERS

Name.	Sex.	Age.	Wide.	Average.	Narrow.	Relation.
B. T.[1]	F.	37	W.	....	....	} Sisters
N. U.	F.	35	W.	....	....	
N. D.	F.	25	W.	....	....	} Sisters
E. D.[2]	F.	15	....	A.	....	
L. N.[3]	F.	18	....	A.	....	} Brother and sister
Q. N.	M.	10	W.	....	....	
G. B.	M.	19	....	A.	....	} Brothers
I. B.	M.	14	W.	....	....	
N. G.	F.	23	W.	....	....	) Sisters
B. G.[4]	F.	20	....	A.	....	} Not fully developed, backward
N. N.	F.	33	....	A.	....	} Sisters, both hysterical Auras
I. N.	F.	22	....	A.	....	
Q. I.	M.	5	....	A.	....	} Brother and sister
O. I.	F.	7½	....	A.	....	
O. N.	F.	23	W.	....	....	} Sisters
N. N.	F.	12½	W.	....	....	
H. K.	F.	29	W.	....	....	} Sisters
E. E.	F.	20	W.	....	....	

As temperament is one of the inherited attributes, it becomes almost a certainty that young children do inherit Auras varying in different degrees which will be retained more

---

[1] The Outer Aura in each of these women is wider on the right than on the left.

[2] Not wider than usual for her age.

[3] Has had one or two epileptic fits, but not for two years.

[4] May be wide in two or three years' time. See Appendix.

or less unaltered during the whole of their lives, unless disease should cause some modification. As might be expected from what has been said above concerning heredity, it will be found that Auras of quick and intelligent children, however young and untrained, will be more extensive than those of the dull and phlegmatic, although the latter may have the advantage in physique. The former, too, will probably have Auras larger and the latter smaller than the average. With adults much the same thing pertains, as the finest Auras envelop the most intelligent people, and small ones surround persons who are dull, or of a low intellectual type. This is not merely seen around their bodies, but becomes more marked round their heads; and is more noticeable among men than women, as the Auras of the former do not develop to the same extent round their bodies. The Auras encircling women are much more variable; but the finest specimens will invariably be found encircling those who are naturally intelligent and slightly excitable, but who have no tendency to neurotic complaints. It, however, may be interesting to observe that the most extensive Auras we have up to the present time seen, belonged to a healthy woman who was naturally quiet, but by no means phlegmatic. In the above descriptions perfect health is taken for granted; and it is interesting to remember that it is only the Outer Aura that shows variations, while the Inner remains stationary.

This is only one phase of the question, and the other is much harder to describe, and probably more important, viz., the texture. It will almost always be found that the Inner Aura will be seen to be more distinctly marked and broader in persons of both sexes who are naturally robust and in good health, but is more faint in weakly subjects, showing that it is the bodily and not the mental powers which are the chief energisers of this portion of the Aura.

As is reasonable to suppose, the Outer Aura of men has a coarser grain than that of women; but, after allowing for this, fineness and transparency may be considered a higher type than coarseness and dullness. Later on it will be shown that the more grey there is in the colour of the Aura, the more dull or mentally affected is the owner.

Education is a factor which ought, theoretically, to have an immense influence on the Aura by its refining influence; but the changes induced by it are so delicate as to be imperceptible by our present means of examination. Nevertheless, it is extremely probable that it has produced a congenital effect through heredity.

The influence of heredity and temperament upon the Aura is one of the most fascinating parts of this subject, and at the same time it does not require a prophet to foresee that an inquirer in this direction is likely to reap a rich harvest.

CHAPTER II

Iᴛ is now time to turn our attention to the subject of the structure of the Aura. There is no doubt about its being a composite phenomenon. There are three divisions of the Aura, not including the rather supposititious Ultra Aura mentioned a little later on, which are the subjects of our investigations. They will be called the *Etheric Double*, the *Inner Aura*, the *Outer Aura*.

The Eᴛʜᴇʀɪᴄ Dᴏᴜʙʟᴇ. — Immediately the Aura was observed, one prominent feature attracted attention, which at first was regarded as an optical illusion, but on further investigation proved to be a reality. The Etheric Double, as seen through various screens, is a dark band adjacent to, and following exactly the contour of the body, separating the latter from the cloud or true Aura. It is, as a rule, from one to three-sixteenths of an inch in width, rarely more, and keeps the same breadth all round the body. It varies in size with different people, and also with the same person under altered conditions. Sometimes it is so conspicuous that it can be seen with the most transitory glance; at other times a very careful examination is necessary for its perception, while not infrequently a special screen is imperative for its detection. In some instances, where there is a difficulty in distinguishing it, the Aura proper apparently reaches right up to the body; but even then close observation will show a difference in structure, and the details can be brought out by the help of coloured screens. The screens employed in the following experiments were red, blue, and green, obtained from Messrs. Wratten and Wainwright, the same as employed for tricolour photography; and in addition to these a yellow screen was used. The blue is too dark, and can be replaced with advantage by a lighter one made of methyl blue. The red screen absorbs all the spectrum from near D downwards, transmitting only the red, orange, and yellow. The blue only allows the spectrum from G downwards to be visible, while the green obliterates the whole of the spectrum except the part lying a little below D to about half way between F and G. The yellow screen cuts off the blue and violet. These results were obtained by means of a small pocket spectroscope, and are only roughly, but yet sufficiently accurate for our purpose.

For the following experiments any part of the body can be utilized, but perhaps the most convenient part is the arm or hand, as the investigation is necessarily a prolonged one, longer than a patient will care to remain uncovered. As soon as the patient has been arranged in a good position, it will be advisable for the observer to look at the light through a dark spectauranine screen for a minute, so that, if possible, he may perceive the Aura without the intervention of a light screen. The inability of seeing the Aura without using a light screen does not entirely debar the observer from performing the following experiments; but he must not expect to see the details to the same extent as if he were able to work without a screen. Of course, for these experiments it will be necessary to choose a subject whose Etheric Double is as well marked as possible; but when once they have been performed, repetition will not be required, as it does not appear that any practicable benefit can be derived from them during the inspection of a patient.

EXPERIMENT 1.—Let the observer inspect the arm and hand of a patient held in front of a black background, through a blue screen. He will see the Etheric Double has a dark band without any striation or granules, adjacent to the body and quite distinct from the Aura proper.

EXPERIMENT 2. — Replace the black background by a white one, and regulate the light accurately, when the Etheric Double will appear as a dark line.

EXPERIMENT 3.—Employ a green instead of a blue screen. Against the black background the Etheric Double will be seen as a dark line, but not so clearly as when the blue screen was employed. The Aura is also visible, but not so distinctly.

EXPERIMENT 4.—When the same screens are used with the patient's arm before a white background, the Etheric Double is dark in a subdued light.

EXPERIMENT 5.—If the yellow screen be employed, the Etheric Double still remains dark either against a black or a white background.

EXPERIMENT 6.—Frequently, when examined through a dark red screen, the Etheric Double will remain as a dark band round the body, similar to, but more marked than when screens of other colours are used. Occasionally it will appear, instead of a dark void space, finely granular with a tendency to striation. Even when lineated the appearance between it and the Inner Aura (to be described in the next chapter) is very unlike, both in texture and colour.

EXPERIMENT 7.—When the Etheric Double is inspected against a white background through a dark carmine screen, it will retain its dark hue. Through a light carmine screen with a properly adjusted light, it will become rose colour, quite distinct from the carmine shade the white background has taken. When carefully examined, it will appear finely lineated, and the striæ are the coloured part.

The use of coloured screens has been found absolutely requisite for the detection of certain constituents, as well as for the elucidation of some of the attributes of the Aura; so a few words about their action upon different colours will not be out of place, although at first sight they may appear elementary. Since all colours behave similarly, *red* alone will be considered in detail.

1st. Upon looking through a dark red screen all white objects will appear red, red objects become lighter in shade, and all other colours seem darker. This can be clearly seen, if in ordinary daylight a piece of white and a piece of black paper be placed side by side, and upon them be laid a strip of red paper of a moderate shade, half on the one and half on the other. When they are examined through a dark red screen, the red paper will be found to have lost nearly all its colour, and the contrast between it and the black paper will be increased, while it will approximate to the colour of the white paper.

2d. Keep the paper in the same position, and view them through the light red screen.

The red paper will then have a darker tint, but the contrast between it and the white paper will remain unaltered, each having gained more red colour in the same proportion. Theoretically, the red paper ought to show out more against the black, but the result depends upon the purity of the black. Should, however, the red paper have a very dark shade, the contrast between it and the black paper will remain unaltered, while that between the red and the white papers will be lessened. The reason is obvious, when we recollect that while daylight is composed of all the colours of the visible solar spectrum, an object appears white when it reflects the whole of these colours equally, but becomes coloured when it reflects only a certain portion of the spectrum, absorbing the remainder.

In the majority of cases the object is only capable of absorbing a limited quantity of light, so that it reflects, with its own coloured rays, more or less white light. The shade of the colour depends upon the proportion of these coloured rays to the white mixed with them, and is really a quantitative expression. If the white light which is being reflected by the coloured object, has those rays, that are similar to the ones absorbed by the object, abstracted by any method, then the object will have a darker hue. This is what is effected by using a coloured screen.

As daylight is limited in quantity, a dark red screen will absorb the whole of it, with the exception of the red rays which are transmitted through it to the eyes. These rays are also limited in quantity. In the above experiment the white paper reflects practically all the daylight falling upon it, therefore it must also reflect the red rays. These are the only rays not absorbed by the red screen, therefore the white paper, when seen through the red screen, must appear as intense a red as possible. The red paper, if not too dark, reflects red rays, mixed with a large proportion of others, which are absorbed by the red screen. The main difference between the action of the red and the white papers, as seen through the red screen is that the former absorbs a portion of the white light which, had it been reflected (as it is by the white paper), would have been absorbed by the screen, thus causing the red and white papers to appear alike. When a light red screen replaces the dark one, all the red rays will be transmitted with the addition of a large quantity of other rays of the spectrum, so that the red paper will have its colour deepened by being seen through this screen. It is necessary to bear in mind that this light red screen will act in precisely the same manner in a dim light as the dark one does in the bright. This fact must be remembered whilst choosing screens for the intensification of the Aura. When these experiments are repeated, the result may possibly not be exactly the same as stated, on account of different shades being used and of the purity of the colours together with the quantity of the light employed, but the principle will remain.

One other experiment is required. Look at a red hot coal, either in the dark or in the light, through a red screen of any shade, it will be seen that the red colour of the coal will be intensified, as it is self-luminous and thus colour is added to colour by absorption of the emitted white light. As has already been noticed, all colours, with the exception of red, will appear either dark or even black when seen through a red screen, according as a part or the whole of the light is absorbed. Should the red screen be not sufficiently deep to absorb the whole of the intrinsic coloured rays reflected by the object, then this object will not merely be darkened, but will have its colour changed by the admixture of the red possessed by the screen.

By these experiments, it may fairly be concluded that the Etheric Double is quite transparent, and surrounds the body closely. When observed under favourable circumstances it is distinctly striated, with very delicate lines of a deeper hue than the surrounding and apparently homogeneous stroma. It seems very probable that the whole of the Etheric Double receives its tint from these coloured lines. The colour is a beautiful rose, which certainly contains more blue than there is in carmine. It is extremely difficult to understand how the rose tint can be seen against the white background when coloured by the carmine screen, and as yet no explanation has been forthcoming, unless it is self-luminous, but so slightly, that, under ordinary circumstances, it is imperceptible. The granular appearance, mentioned in Experiment 6, is evidently due to imperfect differentiation, the surroundings not being quite favourable, as we have never been able to detect them against a white background.

Up to the present time, no attributes or changes in the Etheric Double have been found which are in any way likely to be a help in diagnosis. This being so, together with the frequent difficulty of its detection, we consider that the time that must of necessity be spent upon its differentiation will be more usefully employed in other ways, as the patient will naturally object to his inspection being prolonged beyond certain limits.

CHAPTER III

THE INNER AND OUTER AURAS

THE Aura proper will be found lying just outside the Etheric Double. For some time we were obliged to consider it to be indivisible, although the part nearest the body was manifestly more dense and had a different texture from that further off; nevertheless, the one appeared to shade into the other too gradually to be treated separately. After experimenting for some time, we have found it possible to divide the Aura into two distinct divisions, by means of different screens other than those containing spectauranine. These parts are the Inner and the Outer Auras. The new screens have made a great addition to our knowledge by opening up a new field of observation in disease, and by affording an explanation of several phenomena which were previously inexplicable.

The most useful screen, besides the ordinary spectauranine ones, are A, a dark carmine, B, a light carmine, and C, a pale blue (methyl blue). They are especially valuable to the observer, who has gained the power of seeing the Aura without the intervention of any spectauranine screen. After the patient has been investigated in the usual manner, his Aura may be examined through C. By its means the two Auras may be clearly separated: the Inner will appear more dense and generally more granular, having its outer margin defined, but its general structure hardly differentiated. The Outer Aura stands out clearly, and its distal border can be distinguished with tolerable accuracy, so that its size and shape can be noted. Next, the screen B may be employed, when the Outer Aura will be diminished or entirely obliterated, according to the amount of light admitted and the tint of the screen.

These factors ought to be so arranged that the two Auras may be visible, in order that the width of the Inner Aura, as seen through the screen C, may be corroborated.

At this stage the structure of the Inner Aura can sometimes be discerned, but generally only indistinctly. The last step is to view the Aura through the dark carmine screen *A*, when it will be necessary to admit much more light. It might fairly be conjectured that the screen *A* cuts off some of the Inner Aura, in addition to the whole of the Outer Aura. However, it has been found, after repeated trials, that such does not seem to be the case if the light has been properly regulated; and it is especially to avoid this error that the breadth of the Inner Aura has been previously determined by the screens *B* and *C*. The Inner Aura, as seen through the dark carmine screen, is usually two to four inches in width, according to the age and individuality of the patient, being perhaps relatively wider, although in reality narrower, in a child than in an adult.

In health the boundaries are distinguished by the distance to which the striæ reach, as can be seen through the carmine screen. As a rule, the breadth is practically equal over the head and trunk, being sometimes, but not always, slightly narrower down the limbs. Occasionally, both in males and in females, the Aura will become more coarse and wider locally; but, as lineation can be made out, although it may be with difficulty, there can be no doubt of the increase of breadth. This is quite different to what takes place in local disturbances. The most common position for this enlargement is by the waist as a woman faces the observer, and the next is the small of the back in men; but, when a granular appearance is seen here in women, it is generally pathological, and will be described later on. In the latter sex there is often an increase in front of the breast and abdomen, which will be explained in the chapter devoted to pregnancy.

As a rule the Inner Aura follows the contour of the body, having its proximate border in juxtaposition to the Etheric Double, or often apparently to the body itself. The outer margin is free and irregularly crenated with large curves. The structure is obviously granular, but the granules are so arranged as to look striated, and are exceedingly fine. The striæ are parallel to one another, running at right angles to the body, but have never been seen to possess any intrinsic colour. They appear to be collected into bundles, having the longest ones in the centre and the shortest on the outside, with a rounded margin. The marginal bundles are massed together, and their shape causes the crenated outlines. In some cases the striated appearance is seen without the slightest difficulty, while in others it can only be detected by a careful arrangement of the light, and the choice of a suitable screen. With care the lineation can always be made apparent when the patient is in good health, but in ill health it is otherwise.

Whenever this Aura encroaches upon the Etheric Double, it will almost obliterate it; and this fact again forces upon us the question, whether its granules are not always in the Etheric Double, notwithstanding their invisibility, or whether they are driven by some force emanating from the body to some distance, so as to leave the Etheric Double free from any granules, and therefore quite transparent. In the latter part of the previous chapter, this question was considered when the patient was in good health; and the conclusion arrived at was, that the Etheric Double does not contain any material. Ill health, however, alters the conditions, and it seems to be highly probable that then the granular substance of the Inner Aura does invade the Etheric Double. This will be discussed hereafter.

The Outer Aura commences where the Inner leaves off, and spreads round the body to a variable distance. It has no absolutely sharp outline, but gradually vanishes into space, although it is, as a rule, sufficiently defined for measurement. This statement is, however, hardly correct, because occasionally, under very favourable circumstances, an exceedingly faint haze can be seen extending outwards a very long distance, which gives the impression that we are aware of its presence, but are not quite able to distinguish it. This very elusive portion of the Aura is most probably a continuation of the Outer Aura; because, on all occasions in which it has been noticed, the periphery of the Outer Aura has been more indefinite than usual. It has only been noticed when the patient has an unusually extensive Aura, but may simply be an ordinary component which is too delicate to be often seen. For the sake of reference alone, we have called it the *Ultra-Outer Aura.*

The size and shape of the Outer Aura has already been fully described in Chapter I. It consists of a faint cloud and appears entirely structureless, capable of being illuminated, but not luminous. Very shortly after the commencement of our observations, rays, or streams, or patches of brightness were noticed emanating from various parts of the body. These projections often suddenly appear, then as quickly vanish, while others may remain visible during the whole time of our inspection. The ordinary manner of their occurrence is for one part of the Aura to become brighter and generally more dense. Commonly, rays are colourless, but they may be tinged with different hues. As far as is known at present, these rays possess no diagnostic value, but indirectly they are very important. They may be divided into three groups: *1st.* Rays appearing in and surrounded by the Aura itself, being entirely separated from the body. In this case they often look like bright patches and nothing more. *2d.* Rays proceeding from one part of the body to another. *3d.* Rays projected straight out from the body into space.

The first group of rays consists of patches lighter than the surrounding Aura, but enveloped by it. They are always seen to be in close proximity to the body, but not quite touching it. In their most common form they are elongated, with the long axis running parallel to the body. Their sides can usually be seen quite distinctly, but their ends often fade gradually into the adjacent Aura. For the most part, when present they remain visible during the whole of the observation, but occasionally they suddenly vanish. Had it not been for this latter property, these patches would have been more appropriately placed under the heading of alterations of the Inner Aura. For a long time the origin of these patches was a great puzzle; but directly the Outer and the Inner Auras could be made out as distinct phenomena, one portion of the difficulty disappeared, as these patches were found to lie entirely within the Inner Aura, and through their whole length have their margins, as a rule, exactly coincident with those of the Inner Aura, while their ends are usually contracted and become less bright.

The explanation of the insularity of these

patches is, that they are merely alterations of the Inner Aura, being bounded on the proximate border by the Etheric Double, and on the distal by the Outer Aura. When examined through the dark carmine screen *A* this portion of the Inner Aura seems entirely to have lost its striated appearance, and instead looks granular. The granules of which it is composed are, in some instances, much coarser than in others; and the brightness is often commensurate with their size. When the patch is evanescent, the granules are commonly fine; and, as the patch becomes more lasting, the tendency of the granules is towards coarseness. As these granules must be referred to when considering the Aura in disease, it will be convenient to divide them into *fine*, *medium*, and *coarse*.

Persistence of these patches during the whole of the observation is, certainly, *prima facie* evidence of their having a prolonged existence; and, then, they are more often than not the sign of some local disturbance.

Until quite recently no striæ of any kind had been perceived in them; but, in Case 40, the Aura of a pregnant woman whose fœtus was dead showed, in an unquestionable manner, the physiologically fine striæ in front of the whole sternum; while over the upper part of the distended abdomen the Inner Aura was coarsely lineated, and the lower half had a common pathological granular appearance, all these variations being visible at the same time. These patches never seem to be coloured.

The rays of the second group are, perhaps, the most brilliant of all, and can be observed emanating from any part of the body, running to any other, provided that the two parts be sufficiently near each other and the angle between them be not too great. For example, when the arm is held away from the body, one or more rays may connect them. Here they seem to proceed from the body towards the arm, rather than the reverse way, because the rays are generally perpendicular to the body and take a different angle to the arm. Another good example is obtainable when the patient stands with his hands on his hips and his elbows outwards—a ray appears from the axilla to the wrist. A similar effect can be obtained if the observer holds his hand at a short distance from

any part of the patient, when rays will inter-
vene between the two.   Once, when this experiment was being tried, a ray emitted from the
hand of one person towards the hand of another
was a bright yellow, changing in a few seconds
to a liquid ruby colour.

Rays of the third group are apparently projected at right angles from the body into space,
without any deviation.   Frequently they are
only visible as far as the Outer Aura extends,
but of course brighter.   However, it is not uncommon to see them in the situation where the
Ultra-Aura is supposed to exist.   Whether they
stretch beyond this point of the Aura it is impossible to ascertain, as it is not known how far
the Aura extends.   As the rays proceed outwards they gradually fade into the invisible.
The sides of the rays are generally, if not. always, parallel, and rarely appear fan-shaped,
although after extending some distance they
become pointed as the ends fade away.   This is
especially the case when they issue from the tips
of the fingers.

A straight line perpendicular to the body is
evidently the natural direction of the rays; but

under extraneous influences they may be deflected and proceed at any angle from the body, but in no instance have we seen them curve. It is very easy to watch this phenomenon, as rays emanating from the tips will appear as a continuation of the fingers as long as there is no attractive substance near. But if another hand is held about six or eight inches away and moved about, all the rays proceeding from one to the other will be in straight lines, although from the movement the angles between them and the hands will be constantly altering, but there will never be the slightest sign of any bend.

An exactly similar condition can be produced if the observer holds his hand near a ray given off from any part of the patient's body. The size of the ray varies much, and is dependent, to a large extent, upon its position. For example, rays proceeding from the shoulders are almost always broad, whilst those emitted from the finger-tips rarely exceed one and a half diameters of the digits. Although rays have been seen emanating from every part of the body, when the patient has been standing in favourable positions for their perception, yet, none have ever been noticed proceeding directly from him towards the observer. This is accounted for by the extreme transparency of the rays making their visibility dependent upon a suitable background—flesh colour is a very poor background owing to the want of contrast—while the difficulty of seeing them is further increased by their being foreshortened. On the other hand, the ordinary black background is very efficient; for, when the rays are silhouetted against it, they are made as distinct as possible. Even though the rays proceeding directly from the patient to the observer are invisible, yet they make their presence known by frequently causing an alteration on the complementary coloured band, as will be described in a later chapter.

Besides the ordinary bluish grey colour, red and yellow have been noticed tingeing the rays, so that it is not at all improbable that the rays may possess all the colours of the spectrum. They have one striking peculiarity, namely: that in no instance have the rays been seen to diminish the adjacent Outer Aura, either in density or in brightness, so that they can hardly be considered to arise from that Aura. As their structure resembles that of the Inner Aura, the conclusion is forced upon us that the two have a common origin, viz., the Body; in short, that a ray is only a lengthened out fasciculus of the Inner Aura (page 80).

The Aura has been searched for constantly in the dark without the slightest sign of its being observable, proving that it is not luminous to the ordinary perception. Visibility is derived, as in other non-luminous bodies, from the reflection of light from some extraneous source, the best results being obtained from diffused daylight graduated to the proper extent. It has been our endeavour, but without much success, to ascertain whether one part of the spectrum showed the Aura more plainly than another. It can be seen through red, yellow, green, and blue screens to different extents, varying, of course, with their depth of colour. One very valuable detail, however, becomes more apparent when the red screen (page 77) is employed, viz., the striæ of the Inner Aura.

Another effect of the same screen is that it

sometimes imparts to the Inner Aura a different
tint, a more pure red than that of the carmine
screen.   For the same purpose we called to our
aid photography, hoping to obtain some information by means of panchromatic plates and
others dyed for the Ultra red rays, and ordinary
ones for the Ultra violet, with different coloured
filters.   Unfortunately, however, the results
were negative, owing to the inordinate expo-
sures necessary under the conditions thought
to be advisable.   Nevertheless, we are inclined
to think that the vibrations of the Aura lie
outside the ordinary visible spectrum; and this
opinion is strengthened by the fact that the
Aura would necessarily have been recognized
a long time ago by a number of people who
possess ordinary eyesight, if the rays lay within
the visible spectrum; while at the same time it
has been universally accepted that clairvoyants
are the only people capable of discerning it.

At first sight the cloudlike appearance might
suggest that the Aura was some form of vapour.
This is highly improbable, for the following
reasons: The Aura remains stationary, whether
the patient is hot or cold.   Vapour, if exuded

from the body and warmed, would rise in the
cooler air. The only conditions that could possibly make it stationary (if it were a vapour)
would be similar ones to those governing the
cloud banner seen on the mountain peaks where
the exact amount of vapour is generated as is
lost by diffusion and evaporation. In the latter
case any change of the wind will alter the shape
of the cloud, but no amount of draught or
movement of the body changes in any way the
Auric cloud. Its structure is so delicately fine
that, comparing it to an ordinary mist, would
be analogous to the comparison of the finest
cambric to coarsest canvas.

When all the different aspects of the Aura
are considered, no other conclusion seems possible, except one of the following two: The
first is a most improbable theory, so improbable
that it would not have been mentioned had we
not found hints of it, viz.: "that the Aura
is an integral part of the covering of the body,"
which may be looked upon in the same light
as the skin. If this were so every time anything touched the body the Aura would be
compressed or forced asunder and immediately

close up again, and it could have no protective influence upon the body; neither has it, so far as we can discover. Besides, it would be difficult to imagine how the rays so often seen in the Aura could possibly be generated in it, or what would be their use.

The second theory, most probably the correct interpretation of the Aura, is that it consists of a "force emanating from the body, which, like all forces, is invisible in itself, but which becomes perceptible by means of its action on the Ether, or Atmosphere." Whether this supposition is true or not, it certainly deserves careful consideration.

The first question which naturally arises, is whether there are any other instances of force proceeding from substances making themselves visible in the surrounding medium in the form of a haze ? It is by no means necessary that the force should be exactly similar to the one issuing from the body. Fortunately, Magnetism, Radio-activity, and Electricity (whether static or from the poles of an open galvanic cell) will supply three different kinds of force, all producing analogous results; and they can be seen under conditions similar to those that make the human Aura visible.

It is by no means as easy to see the *Magnetic Cloud* as the Human Aura. In order to obtain the best results, care must be taken in the selection of the background, which must be perfectly smooth and black. The illumination ought to be diffused, and at the same time it is better not to place the magnet opposite the source of light. It might reasonably be expected that the visible cloud would exactly follow the magnetic lines of force; but, as far as has been seen at present, such is not the case, although very likely the discrepancy between the two will vanish directly the haze can be more clearly perceived.

Before commencing an observation, the experimentalist will find it advantageous to look at the light through a dark spectauranine screen quite double the time he is in the habit of doing before the examination of the human Aura; subsequently, no change of procedure is requisite. The magnets used were a six inch horseshoe that had lost a large portion of its power, and an eight inch bar magnet that had been blackened all over. These were chosen in preference to an Electro-magnet, the latter being composite and consequently not so suitable for the present purpose. When the horseshoe magnet, closed by its armature, is inspected, a haze about half an inch wide will be seen encircling it evenly, and the central space will also appear cloudy. Directly the armature is removed, a great alteration takes place. There will still remain a haze round the magnet, but this will be seen to extend and become more dense by the poles, commencing about an inch lower down and culminating a short distance beyond them. A similar change occurs in the central space; but, as the space is a fixed dimension, the cloud merely becomes more dense. From the poles themselves rays project into space, often being visible for several inches.

The rays emanating from the south pole have little tendency towards expansion, while those originating from the opposite pole become slightly fan-shaped, and the two sets amalgamate about an inch and a half beyond the poles. When a bar magnet is examined in the same manner, the cloud will be seen surrounding its length, but becoming broader and denser as it approaches the poles. The rays projected from one pole are uninfluenced by those from the other pole, as these are as far from each other as is possible and thus allowing their arrangement to be accurately observed. It will now be seen that the rays coming off from the south pole are almost straight, while those emitted from the north pole are distinctly fan-shaped, apparently because the rays given off from the sharp edges of the ends are at a different angle from those proceeding from the plain surface. Suppose a tin tack be placed point outwards on the pole of a magnet, the mist will be brighter by the side of the nail and will concentrate at the point. The colour of the magnetic cloud is bluish, and can be intensified by the intervention of a very light blue screen free from any grey.

When a radio-active irregular crystal of Uranium Nitrate, which measured one inch in length and half in breadth at the widest part, was viewed in the same way as has just been described for a magnet, a haze was seen surrounding it. The haze was more concentrated at the smaller end. The colour was yellow and more clearly seen through a light yellow screen, while a blue one lessened or obliterated it according to the depth of colour. It is very interesting to note that when the crystal was placed near a magnet, there was a mutual attraction of the clouds surrounding the two bodies, each of which seemed to have extended further than they did when apart. Moreover, the two hazes could be seen (quite easily owing to their different colours) to interpenetrate one another for a short distance, and then were gradually lost as separate colours. Whether this is due to their intrinsic hues becoming too faint for perception, or whether they absolutely blend, we have been unable to determine.

As every one is conversant with the luminous cloud around the point of an electrified body, it will be quite unnecessary to say anything about it, as it has no connection with the present subject. However, the poles of a galvanic cell, when disconnected, are in a similar static state, but most people cannot distinguish any haze around them. This will become visible when examined in the same manner as the magnetic cloud. As might be expected the haze surrounds any conductor which joins the two poles. If a piece of wire be connected with the zinc element, and another piece with the carbon of a cell, and these two wires are arranged so that they shall be parallel with each other and about two inches apart, the whole intervening space will become nebulous.

Suppose, now, a non-conductor be placed between them, the cloud will no longer be so diffuse, but will concentrate around the two wires. The galvanic haze is bluish, intensified by a light blue screen. It is much coarser in grain than the haze from the Uranium Nitrate crystal, which in its turn is not nearly so fine as the magnetic aureole. It would be out of place to recount any more experiments, as sufficient have been quoted for the purpose of proving that a haze exists around some objects, in which there resides an energy—latent to our usual perception—which energy, however, can, under favourable conditions, be seen to react upon the surrounding medium. In the case of magnetism the force is supplied, according to the usually received opinion, by the peculiar arrangement of molecules, generally termed polarization. The galvanic haze depends upon chemical action taking place within the cell; while the radio-active cloud of the Uranium Nitrate crystal is evidently due to the disintegration of the atoms. It is more than probable that the force giving rise to the human Aura is quite distinct from the above three; and it is more likely than not that there is more than a single force at work—one producing the Outer and the other the Inner Aura. Obviously there is a great similarity between all these clouds, because they are mutually attractive, and possess in common one great peculiarity, that neither the north nor the south poles of a magnet, the positive nor the negative poles of a galvanic cell seem to differ in their attractive power; or, at least, the modification is so slight as not to be discernible.

The force or forces giving rise to the human Aura are most probably generated in the body in some such way as the nervous force. We cannot believe that these two Auras are the product of only one force, for it is to be remembered, *firstly*, that the Inner Aura has a rudimentary structure, being striated; that its borders are fairly well marked, and also that rays proceed from it. *Secondly*, the Outer Aura is entirely nebulous, with an ill defined outer edge, the visible proximate margin of which coincides with the distal border of the Inner Aura; and, again, that in no case as yet have rays been observed commencing in this one passing through to the other. This opinion is strengthened by the fact that the outer margin of the Inner Aura is crenated, showing that the intensity of the force producing it is a little variable; and, the ordinary rays being due to a greater display of the same force, it stands to reason that, if the Outer Aura were derived from this one, it, too, would have a very irregular margin, especially when projecting beyond all the rays; but such is not found to be the case.

Another circumstance pointing to the same conclusion is that the Outer Aura becomes much more developed in females from the age of puberty upwards, around the body, than in males, without any corresponding increase of

the Inner Aura. We are compelled to the conclusion that there must be two forces, one
which originates the Inner Aura, to be called
No. 1 Auric force, or, for shortness sake, 1 AF;
another producing the Outer Aura, to be
termed *No. 2 Auric force*, abbreviated to 2 AF.
If, however, there be only one force, and the
two Auras are only two manifestations of it,
still, for practical purposes, it will be advantageous to treat the subject as if two forces
were present.

1 AF acts apparently very intensely within
a prescribed area, and is, to a certain extent,
under the influence of the *will*, which can cause
a projection of the Aura as visible rays for
some perceptible distance, and very likely much
further than is perceived. Besides, rays are
evolved unconsciously, through the local augmentation of the force. This affords a solution
to the problem that greatly puzzled us whilst
experimenting with the mechanical forces of
the N rays. The difficulty then was that
sometimes a large deflection of our instrument
was obtained; in fact, often too large for measurement, even if the force had to pass through

all kinds of obstacles; at another time, under exactly the same physical conditions, the results were negative. Now, it can be easily understood that a deflection of the needle took place whenever one of these rays fell upon it; and, when there was no ray, the needle remained stationary.

We ceased experimenting by this method, after having come to the conclusion that, however interesting the result might turn out to be, yet there seemed to be no prospect of its being useful for diagnostic purposes, as we had at first hoped. Directly the Aura could be seen we felt that better results could be obtained by studying what was visible, than by working only on the unseen.

2 AF is certainly more mobile, and has a wider range of action than 1 AF; and, as far as has been determined, is entirely independent of the *will* power. Different states of health, either general or local, react upon the forces, and indirectly upon the Auras, altering them, but not necessarily in the same manner. When the affection is local, it is not at all uncommon for all the striæ to disappear from the Inner Aura,

which then presents a more opaque and dense
mass, having a different tint to the neighbouring parts.   It may, however, appear roughly
rayed in a manner very different from the fine
striation of health.   At times a space may look
absolutely devoid of the Inner Aura.   Whenever a change occurs within a large portion of
the body, the Inner Aura may be correspondingly narrower on one side of the body than on
the other; and when this happens, it is always
accompanied by an alteration of texture in the
Inner Aura and, often, by some ill understood
colour change, which will be referred to later
on.   The Outer Aura consequent upon 2 AF
varies much less than the Inner; the colour may
change, but, as a rule, the chief alteration is
in its width, which contracts, but never quite
disappears.   A change over a large area of the
body may cause a complete alteration in the
shape of the Aura, which in some cases is
quite diagnostic.   The Outer Aura may become
narrower, while the Inner Aura retains its normal breadth; but the converse does not occur,
as the Outer Aura never keeps its proper size
after the Inner has shrunk.

The body, as has already been mentioned, has the power of generating Auric rays, which, as well as the Aura itself, possesses the peculiar property of being formed or attracted by outside influences. For example, let the observer hold his hand a short distance from any part of the patient's body, he will find in almost every instance a ray will become visible between his hand and the patient's. Usually, as the first alteration observable, the Auras of both persons become brighter locally, and in a short time a junction is effected producing a complete ray.

It is worthy of notice that these rays can be more easily obtained between points than between large surfaces. For instance, if the observer holds one finger near the side of a patient, a ray will soon appear, but it will certainly be perceived sooner and more definitely near the finger than near the body; subsequently the ray may or may not become equally bright throughout its whole length. Again, if the observer holds his finger the same distance from some pointed part of the patient's body, such as the nose, chin, bended elbow, or fingers, he will notice that the rays will be more quickly generated, and frequently will be brighter.   Thus, if we may use the expression, the Auric potential is greater at points than over a flat surface, having in this respect an analogy to static electricity.

Yet again, if the observer holds a bare arm parallel to the patient's body the intervening Auras will become brighter, and frequently, but not always, blend, showing that a mutual attractive force exists between the two Auras. In all these cases the distance between the patient and the observer should be sufficient to allow one or two inches between their visible Auras.   It is also extremely important that the minds of the two persons should be in as passive a state as possible, in order that the *will* may not affect the Auras.   This is a very good point at which to demonstrate that the Aura is influenced by the *will* power.   The observer can do so by holding his finger some further distance from the patient than in the previous experiments; he must then *will* that a ray should extend from the end of his finger towards the patient.   The ray will soon make its appearance, and it will disappear directly he leaves off *willing*.

As to "How the spectauranine screen enables the Aura to be seen?" It is very important, if possible, to solve the question. Its solution depends upon the constitution of the Aura, the part of the eye most affected in its perception, and, lastly, the action of the screen upon this part. These must be considered in order.

It may be regarded as an axiom "that if any substance emits a force which produces in the adjacent Ether, vibrations corresponding in number and in wave length to the undulations of any part of the visible Spectrum, this substance is "*auto-luminous.*" It does not signify whether the force is self-generated, as in a radio-active crystal, or whether the force has been acquired extraneously, as in the case of luminous Sulphide of Calcium; and, of course, this statement holds good, if this force only produces undulations which are invisible to the ordinary, but which may be seen by persons gifted with some peculiar sight, or by others by means of Instrumental Aid.

Reichenbach, in his "Researches upon Magnetism," gives instances of over fifty sensitives who could see light proceeding from magnets, crystals, etc., in total darkness. Unless all these people were frauds (and there is no reason to suppose them so) they *must* either have possessed a very acute sight, which enabled them to perceive a light too faint to produce any sensation in ordinary men and women, or else the quality of their sight is different, and permits them to perceive phenomena usually invisible. Personally, we think the latter view is correct, as we consider the forces emanating from magnets, crystals, etc., produce vibrations which do nearly but not quite correspond to the undulations of light, both in number and wave length, and in short lie just outside the Solar Spectrum, as usually seen. Perhaps—but this is only supposititious at present—they may be situated within the range of the Lavender Grey. The same may be said of the human Aura. One reason for this is, that if these vibrations are identical with those of any part of the visible spectrum, there are large numbers of people whose sight greatly exceeds the average, and surely some of them would have observed an unusual phenomenon around a magnet, etc., especially as these people are naturally observant on account of the probability that sight is their most developed sense.

This argument would be further strengthened, if it could be shown that clairvoyants are not above the average in keenness of vision for ordinary perceptions. We asked a clairvoyant whether the sight of clairvoyants was, for ordinary purposes, only natural, or whether it was more keen ? He kindly informed us that the gifted sight was in no way connected with the ordinary; and, in fact, some clairvoyants have inferior eyesight. Under these circumstances we may safely conclude that individuals who can perceive the human Aura and the haze around magnets, etc., receive their power not from keenness of sight, but from a faculty to see rays that are not included in the ordinarily visible Spectrum.

If this be not so, in what then does this power consist? All our experiments point to the fact that it is necessary to have only a dim light in which to see the Aura. This may be due partially to the delicacy of the Aura, whose presence is extinguished by a bright light; but the all-important factor is the eye itself. For this reason it will be obligatory to consider the dark adaptation alone. All perceptions of light are due to sensations received through the medium of the rods and cones of the retina; and, for reasons unnecessary to give here, it is usually considered that the most effective action of the cones takes place in a bright light, while they are almost dormant in a dim one. On the other hand, the rods are more sensitive during feeble illumination. Without going into the particulars of their very complicated structure, it will only be necessary to say that this attribute is due probably to the Rhodopsin, or visual purple, which they alone contain. This substance is derived in some incomprehensible manner from the melanin of the pigmented cells of the retina, and is so unstable that light is continually altering its chromatic qualities, different parts of the Spectrum affecting it unequally.

It has been found that the yellowish green rays are the most active, and the red the least so. Under a green light the Rhodopsin becomes purple, violet, and then colourless. As soon as the retina has become accustomed to the dim light, the red end is less apparent, while the maximum intensity is removed to the green, and the blue end becomes brighter. This corresponds to the change seen in the visual purple. When the colour stimulus is slight in the dark adapted state, the object has a grey appearance, which gradually becomes coloured. In our opinion it is the alteration of the visual purple either in quantity or quality that enables people to see the Aura, etc.

If the Aura be observed through a light spectauranine screen without any previous preparation of the eyes, a number of people will be incapable of seeing anything, while a second group will perceive the Aura more or less distinctly. If all these people peer first at the light through a dark spectauranine screen for a short time, and then at the Aura, all will be able to see it—some immediately and the rest within a minute. Of those observers who constitute the second group, a few will be found able, after peering through a dark screen at the light, to distinguish the Aura without the intervention of any screen. These may be classed as a third group. The power thus gained by persons in the third group is only transitory, as it is a very common occurrence for these observers after a minute or two to exclaim "we cannot see anything"; but, as soon as they look at the light through a dark screen for a few seconds, the power returns.

Any one using these screens constantly finds that the effect becomes cumulative, and will be able to perceive the Aura at any time without intervention of any screen, provided the external surroundings are favourable. Nevertheless, he will always find it advantageous, before commencing any serious observations, to look at the light for a few seconds through a dark screen, as he will then discern the Aura more easily and distinctly. This power is gained without any depreciation of the sight; and, so to speak, the eyes have contracted a habit which, by the way, is no explanation of the phenomena. Strange to say, the writer has noticed that when he has not used the screens for a week or two —having been away for a holiday—he cannot perceive the Aura so plainly as before going;

but the power returns again in a very short time. This points to the fact that the cumulative action is not quite permanent.

The above experiments show that Spectauranine has some marked influence upon the eyes. The only part that conceivably is likely to be affected is the visual purple, and if this be the case, it must be either increased in quantity, or altered in quality. Unfortunately the Spectrum, as seen by means of a pocket spectroscope, of the spectauranine does not assist us in any way, except that it shows the yellowish-green to the brightest part, while the orange is entirely and the yellow is to a great extent obliterated. The red is unaltered, and the blue and violet slightly diminished.

The following remarks are completely hypothetical and without proof, but we offer them in default of any other explanation, and ask our readers' kind forbearance if they disagree with them. We do not think an increase in the visual purple alone would be sufficient of itself to account for the perception of the Aura, although it is quite possible that there may be some augmentation in the visual purple. It is more probable that there is some change in its constitution which, after a time by the continuous use of the Spectauranine screen, becomes fairly permanent, and that this alteration enables a person to apprehend rays a short distance beyond the ordinarily visible spectrum. It will be conceded that this is not impossible when it is recollected that the lavender grey is capable of being perceived by some people under favourable circumstances.

CHAPTER IV

COMPLEMENTARY COLOURS

Soon after the discovery of the Aura, a friend called our attention to the fact, that if a light was gazed at, and the eyes turned first to one side and then to the other of any person, the colours of the spectre were often not the same. After having convinced ourselves that this peculiarity did occur, we thought it might be a help in diagnosis, but for that purpose we knew that the investigation by means of complementary colours must be made methodical. We began by gazing at a gaslight for the employment of its complementary colour, not that we thought that such a crude method would be satisfactory, but to discover its defects, so that they might guide us in our future experiments. We noticed that the resulting phantom was not a single colour, as the main portion had one colour, but was surrounded by another quite different. The inconvenience of

114

having to work with two or more colours simultaneously was immediately apparent, an insurmountable difficulty arising from the constant changing of the colours of the spectre, quickly one after the other, an effect caused by the slight movement of the eyes necessary for seeing the image on the two sides of the subject, consequently no accurate results could be obtained. It was felt that if any benefit was to be derived from this process, a monochromatic spectre was essential.   After many experiments we came to the conclusion that pieces of coloured paper answered the purpose better than anything else.

This chapter will be entirely devoted to this problem, viz.: the effect of the Aura upon complementary colours—a more extraordinary property can hardly be conceived.   The change observed is as follows: —When a monochromatic spectre is employed the shade of the colour becomes either lighter or darker under certain conditions.   As may be expected, it is a very difficult and complicated subject to deal with, but we will give the best explanation we can; yet some of the theories may appear farfetched or even heterodox; nevertheless, they are advanced for the want of better hypotheses. As the subject is entirely dependent upon colour-vision some preliminary remarks are required on that process.

It is a generally accepted fact, that there are three sets of colour-sensitive nerves in the eyes, and that all the colours perceived arise from the stimulation of one, two or all of these sets of nerves, either separately or in conjunction. When more than one set of nerves are excited, they are usually unequally stimulated. The true physiological primary colours are those that can stimulate only one set of colour-sensitive nerves simultaneously. One method of ascertaining a person's own personal primary colours, is to press the closed eye, when there will usually be seen small yellow dots all over the field of vision. Intermingling with these are much larger discs of blue, and lastly red points intermediate in size between the yellow and blue discs. The yellow are the most numerous and the blue next in number.

When all the colour-sensitive nerves are excited equally the object is called white, but when unequally it is coloured. We have for many years considered that each person possesses his own primary colours, and accordingly sees a coloured object differently to any one else, but by means of education every one calls the colour by the same name.   For instance let two persons *A* and *B* look at a coloured object, usually designated as a shade of yellow.   This colour might only stimulate one set of colour-sensitive nerves of *A*, and would be to him a pure yellow.   On the other hand with *B*, not merely might the yellow-sensitive nerves be excited, but to a slight extent the blue-sensitive nerves; he would see it as a greenish colour. But as *A* and *B* have both been taught that the colour is a certain shade of yellow, whenever they see it, they will both call it by the same name.   Nevertheless, if *A* saw it with *B's* eyes he would immediately say it was a greenish yellow, while *B*, looking through *A's* eyes, would give it some other name.   Each would be correct.   It follows as a corollary, that every one sees nature in hues different from what his neighbour does.   It is unnecessary to enter more fully into this theory, but according to it the writer's primary colours are, at the present time, red, yellow and blue. Twenty years ago purple took the place of blue. We do not propose to consider any other theories, since this one will do perfectly well for our purpose.

Putting aside for the time being all theories, it will be found that when one set of colour-sensitive nerves is completely fatigued, the observer is, for the time being, colour-blind. If the red-sensitive nerves be the ones exhausted, he will be red-blind, although he will be able to perceive perfectly all the colours that do not contain red; in addition he will see any colour that has a mixture of red, as the hue would be if all the red colour were removed. Taking a simple example, purple would have the appearance of a shade of blue. This artificial colour blindness causes the eyes to become hyper-sensitive to all colours and shades of colours, that do not contain red, as red in an ordinary way helps to obscure a very faint tint of any colour. The following experiment has been tried by several people and will furnish a proof. When a band of light, tinged very faintly with carmine, is thrown upon a white screen from a magic lantern, it will have a certain visibility; but should the observer look for a minute or so, first through a blue or a red glass at the sunlight, he will see the band more plainly or less markedly respectively for a short time. Similar results will be obtained if the eyes be fatigued by looking at a blue or yellow band (*vide* ultra), when the observer becomes temporarily blue-blind or yellow-blind. Were it possible for the perception of two sets of colour-sensitive nerves to be annihilated for a short time, the observer would become perfectly monochromatic.

This, however, is not required for our investigation. In practice it has been found almost impossible by this method to induce simple red, blue, or yellow blindness. Most probably all the colour-sensitive nerves will be partially excited, although one set be almost completely paralysed, and this fact complicates the observations. However, the observation remains true that, "the eyes have become abnormally sensitive to certain shades of colour." Perhaps this may partly explain how it is that a person is enabled to perceive the human Aura after looking at the light for a short time through a spectauranine screen, since his eyes have been made more sensitive to the extreme limit of the spectrum, and most probably even to vibrations lying beyond and totally invisible in an ordinary way.

Every one is aware that if he gaze intently for a short time at a coloured object, and then look at a blank space he will see a spectre of the object similar in shape, but having a different hue. This secondary colour will always be the same, is dependent upon the hue of the object, and is termed "complementary" to the real or "primary" colour. If, for example, a yellow object be gazed at, the colour of the virtual image will be blue, the exact tint being determined by the shade of the yellow employed, and to a certain extent by personal idiosyncrasies. When the observer has looked sufficiently long at the object, the time varying according to the brightness of the light and the steadfastness of his gaze, etc., he will always perceive at first the spectre to have the same hue, but this gradually becomes lighter, and will more frequently than not become blended with a red tint, turning purple or plum-col-

oured.   In these cases it must be remembered
that the complementary colour always includes
a red tint, although at first it is masked by
the intensity of the blue colour.

Should, however, the observer see at first the
purple or plum-coloured tints on the phantom,
he may be sure his eyes have not been completely saturated by the original yellow colour,
or else that there is a larger amount of white
light present than usual.   This shows how requisite it is to be conversant with all the varying tints that the spectre undergoes.   After a
short time the phantom will vanish and may
return with quite altered colours.   For the
present purpose this secondary change may be
neglected, because the use of the complementary colours is not continued long enough to
produce it.   One other fact remains to be borne
in mind, namely; that when the background is
not white, the complementary colour will not
appear in its pure shade, but as if blended with
the tint of the background.   Since the complementary colours are entirely subjective, they
will receive the names of the nearest colours
of paints that could be obtained, these being

accurate enough for all practical purposes. After a large number of experiments had been made with the colours we call our primary ones, we came to the conclusion that these did not give such good results as mixed ones. Numerous trials have shown the following colours to be the most useful:

1. Gamboge having a complementary colour, Prussian Blue.
2. Antwerp Blue, Gamboge.
3. Carmine, Transparent Emerald Green.
4. Emerald Green, Carmine.

However, the Investigator must determine by experiment what colour or colours suit him best.

In actual practice use is made of strips of tinted paper three inches long and three quarters of an inch wide, pasted upon a black cardboard. These are the largest size that can be conveniently employed, since longer ones do not give the complementary colours perfect to the ends. When a patient stands a few feet in front of the observer, these strips will give bands of complementary colours, which when used transversely, will be wider than the body, allowing the ends of the coloured bands that are projected on each side of the body to be compared with one another, and also with that part on the body itself. When used perpendicularly the band will cover the greater length of the thorax and abdomen simultaneously, or if the back is the part under inspection, it will include the greater part of the spine from above downwards.

Directly the patient is ready to be examined by this process, he must be placed in front of a white background opposite the light so as to be illuminated evenly all over, and should there be any shadows upon the background, they must be made equal on both sides. Preferably the light should be greater than when the Aura itself is being inspected, but almost always it will be necessary for the blind to be drawn down. When the patient has been properly arranged, the observer must gaze at one of the coloured strips, keeping his eyes steadfastly upon the spot from thirty to sixty seconds or more according to the brightness of the light.

For this purpose the more brilliant it is, the better, consequently it is as well to pull aside

the blind so that the strip may be fully illumi
nated. Directly he considers his eyes to be
sufficiently colour-blinded, he turns towards the
patient and looks at some predetermined point
on the median line of the body, when (if used
transversely) the complementary coloured band
will be seen reaching right across the body and
partly extending to the background on either
side, all being simultaneously visible. This
allows him to notice variations in the shades
of colour in every part of the band. Of course,
the tints of the parts of the band extended beyond the body can be compared with each
other, but not with the portion on the body
itself. The above method seems a very simple process, but it will require a considerable
amount of practice, and the mastery of one
or two details, trifling in themselves, will assist
greatly in the speed and comfort of the experiment.

First, while looking at the coloured slip, it is
requisite not only to fix the eyes on one particular spot, but to keep this in exact focus the
whole time, as there is a great tendency to blur-
ring which will greatly increase the length of

time necessary for gazing at it.   A slight effort of the *will* is needful for this, but in a short time habit will make the strain almost involuntary.   If this spot on the coloured slip be replaced by a letter or figure, a double purpose will be served, a fixed point and a means of registration will both be gained.   Secondly, a difficulty is experienced when beginning this inspection, in keeping the eyes fixed upon a given spot on the patient's body, owing to the proneness of the complementary coloured band to move, often out of the line of vision and the eyes follow it, thus completely destroying the benefit of the observation.   As soon as the habit of keeping the eyes stationary upon one point has been acquired, the complementary coloured band will remain fairly motionless, and should it move away it will return again to the proper position of its own accord.   As dexterity is only acquired by practice, it is a good plan to train the eyes upon some inanimate object before proceeding to the examination of a human subject.

In the following description, unless otherwise specified, the yellow strip with its blue complementary coloured band will be the colour implied. For brevity's sake the term C. C. will be employed for complementary coloured, and P. C. will mean the primary colour or the colour of the strip gazed at. As, naturally, there are slight variations of the skin and shadows on the body of the patient, the observer ought to notice every modification however insignificant, before commencing inspection with the C. C. band. With care, judgment and a little experience most of the difficulties arising from these causes will disappear. In its simplest aspect the C. C. band projected on a body in good health, will be equal in tint all over, after due allowance has been made for any deviation of the colour of the skin. The extensions of this band on the two sides often, but not always, correspond in hue. These extensions, as would be expected, have invariably quite a different tint from that of the part of the C. C. band lying on the body itself, mainly on account of the colour of the background.

When the extensions of the C. C. band of a healthy subject show a tint on the one side unlike that of the other, the difference is rarely

great.   This diversity of shade is the simplest
form of alteration of the C. C. band, and unless sufficient care has been taken, may be due
to imperfect lighting; however, any doubt
can be dissipated by turning the patient round,
when, if correct, the different tints will have
changed places, being a proof positive that the
alteration is an effect of the Aura itself.   Another very characteristic method when successful, is to notice which extension of the blue
C. C. band has the deeper colour, and then to
gaze at the blue P. C. strip which gives a
yellow C. C. band.   Frequently, but not always, the latter will have a lighter shade where
the blue C. C. band was darker, and vice versa.

One of the chief variations of the C. C. band,
when projected transversely upon the body of a
patient not in good health as he stands facing
the observer is, that one side will be darker
than the other.   When this happens, the two
shades of colour may blend gradually into each
other, or a sharp line of demarcation may divide
them.   In the latter case the division most frequently takes place in the median line of the
body, but exceptions are numerous and the line

of separation may occur any distance to the right or left. If the C. C. band (on one side light and on the other dark) be continued beyond the body, the extension on the light side will have invariably a lighter shade than the extension of the dark portion of the band. The dark part generally overlies some deranged portion of the body, and it will be found that this part has absolutely become darker than the rest of the band. However, the deranged part of the body may cause the C. C. band to become lighter instead of darker.

But slightly different is another variation, in which instead of the C. C. band across half the body being changed in shade, only a patch, large or small, is noticed to be dark or light and wholly surrounded by the natural colour of the band. When the patch is large it occasionally takes the outline of an organ in whole or in part; the small patches not exceeding about an inch in diameter, do not of themselves disclose what organ is affected, although they generally point to some disease or local disturbance and almost invariably to the seat of tenderness or pain. In these instances when the colour change is slight, the variations may constantly be perceived more readily when the colour is fading. So far reference has been made to some part or other of the band which has become either lighter or darker; occasionally, however, the spots are changed in colour (Case 33) as if another hue had been added, while in one or two instances brown (Case 17) has been substituted for the blue in the band.

Four P. C. slips have been chosen, but it will be found that each has advantages not possessed by the other. These advantages are generally dependent upon some obscure cause connected with the patient. For ordinary observations, the P. C. yellow strip giving a blue C. C. band is the most useful, since it is more sensitive to change than the yellow C. C. band, while the latter is especially valuable as a control for the blue C. C. band, owing to its so often being the reciprocal, when there is a local change of tint. There are occasions also when for some incomprehensible reason it is advantageous to work with the yellow C. C. band rather than the blue. Perhaps the most sensitive of all these bands is the green, but unfortunately it does not undergo so many variations as the blue, and the changes are also more fleeting in character. In cases of doubt its delicacy of action sometimes decides a question of fine differences of colour. The choice of a colour for the C. C. band is not very important in the ordinary way, if it be borne in mind that occasionally, owing to individual idiosyncrasies of a patient, better results with one colour than another can be obtained; unfortunately there seems to be no means of deciding which is the best band to employ except by use.

During these experiments the observer will find that his eyes very soon become fatigued, and as no amount of will power can be of any assistance, he will either have to leave off the inspection for a short time, or else change the C. C. band. The former when possible is decidedly preferable, as the other is to a great extent a makeshift to be used when the observation cannot be continued very much longer. Should the latter method be chosen an alternative C. C. band to one previously used will be found the best to employ.

A most pertinent question—one very difficult

to answer now arises.   "What is it that causes
the C. C. band to be altered in colour?''   For
reasons already stated, it seems more than probable that the eyes of the observer are hypersen-
sitive to certain colours after gazing at one of
the P. C. strips, and can differentiate tints so
nearly alike as would baffle ordinary perception.
Theoretically there appear to be four agencies
which can alter the shade of the C. C. band.
Firstly, the skin, secondly, the thickness of the
Aura, thirdly, alteration of texture, and lastly,
the colour of the Aura.   Each of these proposi-
tions must be considered in turn.   After having
made all possible allowances for any variation
of tints which can be appreciated in the ordinary way, it is quite within the bounds of reason
to imagine there may exist hues of the skin
that can only be distinguished under exceptional circumstances.   We have constantly borne
this in mind, and have tried to find some instance that would uphold it, but up to the
present time without any success, so that personally we believe that although possible, it
must be extremely rare, so rare as to be neg-
ligible.   One fact that militates against the

skin being the cause of the change of tint, is that when the C .C. band is discoloured up to the edge of the body, the extension beyond will be similarly affected, being lighter or darker as the case may be. Under no circumstances can the latter change result from the influence of the skin, therefore there is nothing else to which it can be attributed save the Aura, although it seems hardly credible that such transparent, nearly colourless, almost invisible, finely divided matter should have such an effect upon the complementary colours. Secondly: Is the thickness of the Aura sufficient to produce a change in the C. C. band?'' Everything points to a negative answer to this proposition; there is no evidence to lead us to such a conclusion.

As the Aura is a highly attenuated material (we use the word advisedly) it would have to acquire an enormous thickness before it could produce any perceptible alteration in the complementary colour. One case (No. 30, Fig. 21) illustrates this fact in the strongest way. It is that of a woman, who, when standing sideways to the observer, had the Aura over her abdomen quite four times as wide as over the thorax.

Now as she stood facing, no difference could be seen either directly or when the C. C. band was used, since the colour was exactly the same on the thorax as on the abdomen, proving it. It is common to meet with analogous instances during pregnancy when the woman then has the Aura in front of the abdomen three or four times wider than it is before her thorax. In no case has this extra breadth made any difference to the shade of the C. C. band.

The first two theoretical agencies, that can produce a change in the shade of the C. C. band, have thus been discounted, and there remains the third and the fourth, which seem to offer to some considerable extent a solution of the problem. Thirdly: Can a change in the texture of the Aura induce a sufficient alteration in the C. C. band to account for change in its tint ? In Chapter III it has been noticed that the Inner Aura may lose its lineated appearance, and become granulated. This state is met with in persons apparently in good health, but much more frequently during ill health, or when there is some local disturbance of which the details will be described in another chapter.

At the present time all we are concerned with is the query as to whether the gross change of the texture of the Aura can cause an alteration in the C. C. band or not? In certain instances it does seem sufficient; in others its action is nil, and in a third set although it may assist, yet there is another factor at work. Referring to Case 32 it will be found that the patient, as she stood facing the observer, and was examined with the blue C. C. band, had a large patch over the left hypochondrium, darker than the remaining normal portion of the band, and that the extension of the band partook equally of the alteration. When inspected through a dark carmine screen the Inner Aura, by the side of the trunk, showed that this part of the Aura had become coarsely granular between the level of the sterno-xiphoid and the intertubercular planes; and, when she stood sideways, or half sideways, this could be observed in the same region in front of the trunk. In another well marked instance (Case 21), when the C. C. band was projected upon the thorax, it was much lighter on the left side and beyond than on the right.

When this part was examined through carmine screens, the Inner Aura was found to
be granular, but not so coarsely as on Case 32,
and would come under the heading of medium
granulations.   Moreover, in women, a dark
patch has been constantly observed with both
the blue and yellow C. C. band upon the lower
lumbar and sacral regions.   The patch varies
in tint, and the variation in some way seems to
be dependent upon the amount of local pain the
woman suffers during menstrual periods.   Here,
with the carmine screens, the Inner Aura will
always be perceived to be granular, almost always coarse, when the C. C. band has been
darkened, and usually medium or fine when
the band is lighter.   Other instances could be
quoted, but we think that these suffice to prove
that in some cases the granular condition of
the Aura will account for the alteration of the
C. C. band.

On examination of a woman twenty-five years
of age, who complained of having a pain in her
back for over three years, there was seen a wide
ray about three inches long proceeding from
the outer part of the left buttock, which looked

coarsely granular when seen through a carmine screen. Directly she was inspected by means of the C. C. bands, no difference in their shades could be discovered, notwithstanding the use of different colours. This case shows that the altered texture of the Aura, as far as could be ascertained (exactly as in former instances) did not affect the colour of the C. C. band. A similar case, is that of a girl, (Case 23) who had a ray proceeding from the left breast, that was short and thick, and, when examined through a carmine screen looked coarsely granular. When the blue C. C. band was thrown upon the spot from which the ray emanated, it appeared lighter than the surrounding normal band, while with a yellow C. C. band, this same space looked darker than the rest of the band. In this instance there must have been some other cause than the merely granular condition of the Aura to produce the modification of the C. C. band.

To sum up:

(1) When the alteration of all the shades of all the C. C. bands is the same, the granular

state of the Aura is most likely the cause of the modification.

At times, this granular state has no effect upon the C. C. band.

(2) When the C. C. bands are altered, some being made lighter and some darker, there can be no doubt that the change is not entirely due to the granular condition of the Aura, but that some other factor is present.

The fourth, and last agent, namely, "the colour of the Aura" seems to be the only one that will explain all the remaining cases, and it supplies the missing factor in the last example. It may be problematic,[1] but is certainly correct in many instances and gives a good working hypothesis. It is as follows: namely, that the Aura is coloured, although the colours may not be distinguishable by the naked eye. Yet they are sufficiently intense to modify the C. C. band. As presumptive evidence, clairvoyants affirm that they can see the Auras in all colours, and that often a colour may be only local.

Generally the Aura looks to the writer blue,

---

[1] See Appendix.

or blue mixed with more or less grey, or even grey itself. This constant colour is most likely due to the employment of the spectauranine screen and to its long period of action upon the retina after peering through it at the light. Occasionally, even after this preparation of his eyes with the spectauranine screen, the writer has noticed that, when omitting the use of the light screen, the Aura has had a yellowish or greenish tinge. This latter is probably the effect of the admixture of yellow upon the blue. The following phenomenon gives great weight to the above theory. A ray was seen emanating from the forefinger of a man in good health, the ray, at first a lemon colour, changed rapidly to a transparent ruby red. The ray was about one inch in length and half an inch wide. It proceeded straight outwards without any expansion or contraction, and was apparently more dense than the surrounding Aura. Behind was a black background so that it was seen under very favourable circumstances (see page 87).

Now suppose this yellow ray to be projected from the patient's body towards the observer, instead of from the finger, would it have been visible? The surroundings would not be anything like as propitious, because the background would be flesh-coloured instead of black, and the observer could only see it foreshortened as a yellow spot about half an inch in diameter, surrounded and, most likely, overlapped by the Outer Aura. After having carefully considered every point, intensity, density, background, etc., we have come to the conclusion that the ray would have been perfectly invisible to the naked eye, while we have not the slightest doubt about its being visible by means of the C. C. band. With a blue C. C. band the observer would see a spot about half an inch in diameter, darker than the surrounding colour, and if he used a yellow C. C. band, it would manifest itself as a lighter patch.

In this particular instance, given above, if the Aura were inspected when the ray was red instead of yellow, we are still of an opinion that it would be invisible to the naked eye, but with either the blue or yellow C. C. bands it would be plainly seen as a dark spot. As these bands fade away the spot may change its tint, but this would be more probable with the blue band, owing to the range of colours it passes through whilst disappearing. If inspected through a red screen, this spot ought to retain its red hue, but be lighter than the normal colour of the band. It may be added that even if a particular yellow or red ray were visible to the naked eye, it can easily be conceived that the colours might then be a little less bright, yet, could be better seen by the aid of the C. C. band. If in this and similar rays the lines, as they proceed outwards, remain parallel, the spot would be sharply defined, but should they expand, then the edges will be blurred and the colours of the spot and of the C. C. band gradually blend into each other, causing a difficulty in seeing the large, and an impossibility to perceive the smaller ones. This theory will also supply the reason why a patch will appear darker with one C. C. band and lighter with another. In the next chapter will be found a description of gaps in the Aura. These will afford another explanation of the chromatic changes in the C. C. band.

As the forces which produce the Aura act usually at right angles to the body, their local cessation would be an immediate cause of a space devoid of any Aura, and the general result would be towards the formation of cylindrical gaps having their long axis at right angles, and one of their ends in contact with the body (Case 26). When the Auric forces are in complete abeyance at one spot, and acting partly in the surrounding parts, increasing in strength further off from the given spot until they have regained their full power instead of a cylinder being formed, the void space will become conical with its pointed end towards the body (Cases 24 and 25). As might be expected the Aura surrounding these gaps is sometimes, if not always, modified in texture. The following are the data that serve as the interpretation of the changes in the C. C. band in certain instances.

First, the cylinder as seen on a side view will be considered. If the texture of the Aura surrounding it has not in any way become disorganised, theory would lead us to expect a colour change in all the C. C. bands indiscriminately, and that this change would cause the tint to be lighter in shade. In this instance practice corroborates theory. If, however, the Aura surrounding the void space should be affected (especially if it has been made more dense and granular), the alteration in the C. C. band might, and usually would result in the production of a darker shade, and this would hold good for C. C. bands of all colours. Nevertheless it is conceivable, although we have never identified an instance, that the change that has taken place in the Aura might be one of discoloration, and then there would be produced a darker shade in some of the C. C. bands and a lighter tint in others.

Secondly, if the gap in the Aura be conical, and seen in a similar position, the same arguments in the main will hold good, but owing to the shape of the gap, the change of shade in the C. C. band instead of being sharply defined would have a blurred margin, the tints of the spot and the rest of the band gradually blending into each other. It is self-evident that in the whole of this description the colour changes will take place outside the body in the extension of the C. C. band.

It will be shown later on that the defects of

the Aura can only become visible under favourable conditions, and one condition that seems imperative is that the void space should be silhouetted upon a black background. For this purpose the patient should be placed in such a position that the long axis of the cylinder is parallel with the background, as any deviation from this position will obscure it partially or wholly. If the patient turns round so that the axis of the cylinder proceeds from him to the observer, the space devoid of the Aura will be invisible, owing to the fact that it is foreshortened and that the flesh is a very bad colour for a background upon which to examine the Aura. However, the situations of these vacant spaces of the Aura can be detected by means of the band. The appearances of the band will differ according to the size of the defect, and the condition of the adjacent Aura.

If the substance of the Aura all round the gap be unimpaired, the C. C. band will show a sharply defined light spot. If the adjacent Aura has become more dense and granular when the vacant space is large, it may still be seen as a light patch, which ought theoretically to be surrounded by a dark line, but this is a refinement too subtle to be detected in practice. This discoloured patch will be constant with C. C. bands of all colours. If under the same conditions the vacant space be small, we may expect either to see a dark space, or no change whatever in the C. C. band according to the amount of modification that has taken place in the Aura. When the defect is conical, the alteration in the C. C. band will cover a large surface, but the graduation will be so that in all probability no chromatic changes can be detected.

It will be convenient to tabulate the changes of colour induced by the Aura in the C. C. band. The first division will contain the derangement of the Aura over a large portion of the body, and secondly, in contradistinction to be entirely surrounded by the normal colour. This classification, of course, is artificial, but is useful as the former division may include an alteration that can comprise half the circumference of the body, and at the same time the causes and variations are not so many.

1. Alteration of Colour over a large portion of the body.

Separation of the two shades may be. . . .
{
Sharply defined.
Gradual change from one shade to the other.
}

Due to the Aura becoming granular. .
{
Coarse, inducing darker shade.
Medium, usually producing lighter shade.
Fine, usually producing lighter shade or, perhaps, no alteration.
}

Chromatic changes of the Aura problematic.

2. Discoloured patches of various sizes which can be seen entirely surrounded by the normal colour of the C. C. band.

SEPARATION BETWEEN THE TWO SHADES

Patches sharply defined . . . .
{
Circumscribed local derangement with the Auric Force great. A Ray can be seen. Gaps in the Aura. Entire but restricted absence of Auric Forces.
}

Patches gradually blending . . . .
{
Deranged Auric Force, greatest in the centre gradually lessening towards edges. Gaps in the Aura from want of Auric Force which becomes stronger the more distant it is from the centre.
}

Aura when granular
- Coarse, inducing darker shade.
- Medium, usually inducing lighter shade.
- Fine, lighter shade or no alteration.

Chromatic change . .
- Associated the granular state, pure and simple (dark or light change of hue).

CHAPTER V

If the theory be correct that the sources of the Aura are forces generated within the body, and that their action upon the ether is the cause of their visibility, it is reasonable to expect that these forces will not be exactly the same in health and disease. In the former after making allowance for sex and age, the Auras, both Inner and Outer, and most likely the Ultra Outer, are very similar within certain limits, the variations being due to individuality. It is extremely difficult to imagine that any departure from health can occur without in some way influencing one or more of the auric forces, and consequently the Aura itself. If the ailment be only local, then most probably there will be only a local change in the Aura; but should the patient suffer from some general disease the whole Aura is likely to be affected, and, as recovery takes place, it will very probably return

147

to its pristine state. The alteration in the Aura may apparently not be at all commensurate with the illness, as some of the modifications are much too subtle for detection by the crude methods of observations at present available, but it may be taken for granted that future methods of investigation will disclose a greater number and variety of minute defects. The changes most likely to be detected at the present time are variations in the size and shape of the Aura, together with alterations of colour and texture.

The Aura of anyone in good health is invariably symmetrical as he stands either facing or with his back to the observer. Two cases mentioned elsewhere (page 188) are the only exceptions we have met with. Down the front and back of a person standing sideways there is no equality. As long as the proper shape of the Aura is retained there seems to be no means, except experience of telling whether it is large or small, since no standard of size exists. A standard of comparison might possibly be obtained if the Aura of a patient had been previously measured when in good health, but even then it must be remembered that the apparent enlargement or diminution might be only due to some change of texture, as visible size and texture are often associated the one with the other.

For the present we shall confine our attention to instances in which the whole, or a large portion of the Aura are modified in shape from constitutional causes. The first variation from that of a typically healthy Aura is that found in women and girls suffering from hysteria. In this complaint the characteristic form of the Aura of the patient, as she stands facing the investigator, is symmetrical on the two sides, wide by the side of the trunk; but the Aura, instead of as in health gradually diminishing and reaching its narrowest limits not higher than the lower half of the thigh and very frequently much further down, suddenly contracts to its final breadth, either at, or a very short distance from the pubes. As she stands sideways, the Aura in front of the body is the full average or even wider, while at the back it is broad, with a well-marked bulge outwards in the lumbar regions. At this point it contracts very sharply diminishing to its minimum. The contraction takes place at the same level on a side view and from thence proceeds downwards at an even breadth.   Only two cases will be quoted now, as several others must be referred to later on for various purposes.

CASE 13.—I. N., a young woman of twenty-two years of age, a dressmaker, well developed, slightly anæmic, very nervous, complains of being weak, and short of breath.   Her pulse is fluctuating, having eighty to ninety beats a minute when quiet, increasing to one hundred and thirty or more upon the slightest exertion. There are cardiac murmurs which are constantly changing their positions or vanishing entirely. She suffers from *globus hystericus*, which she describes as starting from the umbilicus.   Sometimes she has fainting fits, which last for about a quarter of an hour, during which she declares she is perfectly cognizant of what is going on around her.   Under the administration of a tonic she rapidly improved.   The general colour of her Aura was bluish grey.   The Inner Aura was well marked, lineated, about two inches wide all over her body.   As she stood facing the observer, the Outer Aura was two inches wider than the width of the shoulders. When the hands were placed at the back of the head the Outer Aura was about nine inches wide by the side of the trunk, and diminished rapidly to just below the pubes, where it measured only two and a half inches, the same breadth being maintained down the thighs and legs. As she stood sideways, in front of the trunk it was about three inches, narrowing to two and a half.

At the back it bulged out in the lumbar region to quite seven inches contracting suddenly just below the nates, where it became two and a half inches wide continuing the same breadth downwards. A ray was seen emanating from the right lower ribs about six inches long which passed completely through the Inner Aura and lost itself in the Outer. Another ray came off from the lower dorsal spines, being about three inches wide and six in length. As she stood facing the observer, the Inner Aura on the left side from below the mamma—as far as the lowest rib—was coarse in texture without the slightest sign of striation. When the blue C. C. band was employed perpendicularly down the chest and abdomen, it was even throughout, except just above the pubes where it was darker showing that she was near her menstrual period. This she expected in four days. When the band was used transversely, a dark patch was observed on the right lumbar region which was tender to the touch. At the level of the transpyloric plane the band was even across the body, but the right extension was lighter than the left. The difference in tint was not so marked, as is often the case when the Inner Aura is coarsely granular, locally. There was a dark patch on the two upper dorsal spines; this part was tender and she often had pain there. Nothing further was to be noted.

Girls who are more emotional than they should be, and who are generally described by their relatives as "slightly hysterical," although they may never have suffered from any grave attack, show a great tendency for their Auras to partake, to some extent, of the characteristics of what has been termed the hysterical Aura. On the other hand women not naturally hysterical, who through grave anxiety or trouble have a nervous breakdown, do not

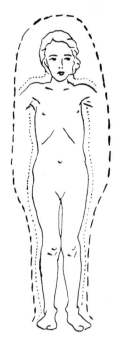

FIG. 14.—Hysterical Aura in a young girl.
Very wide by the trunk for a child.
Compare with Fig. 25.

FIG. 15.—Hysterical Aura in a young girl.
Side view.   Great bulge at back.
Compare with Fig. 26.

show Auras of this peculiar type. A well marked instance is that of the young lady mentioned in Case 35.

Whilst examining some children for the hereditary sizes of the Aura, we came across a most interesting instance of what may be termed the hysterical shape, a very good illustration of the above description.

CASE 14, Figs. 14 and 15.—E. X., a girl, not quite eight years of age, was inspected in July, 1910. She was a bright clever child, but very excitable and had a neurotic parentage on both sides (see Table 1). The Aura was bluish grey in colour. The Inner Aura was about one and a half inches wide all over the body. On the left side it was, for the whole length of the trunk, bright, being a very good instance of No. 1 Ray (page 84). After a short time this brightness diminished and the Aura resumed its natural state. It, however, suggested the appearance of the rays proceeding from different parts of the body, but none were absolutely seen. Round the head the Outer Aura was a little wider than the breadth of the shoulders. When she placed her hands behind her neck, the haze was four inches by the side of the trunk, narrowing to a little less than three at a very short distance below the pubes, whence it descended regularly downwards. It was not, however, easy to determine the exact width, as the margin especially by the lower limbs, was ill defined. When she turned sideways, the Outer Aura was not quite three inches down the side of the body, but at the back it bulged out, from just below the shoulders, to six inches at the lumbar region and curved in sharply a short distance below the nates. The C. C. band was even all over the body. This child had a very wide Aura for her age, which is the more remarkable as all the other members of the family had narrow ones. It also shows as distinctly an hysterical type as it is possible to see in an Infantile Aura.

The next disease to be considered is *Epilepsy*. The Aura of epileptics has a distinct character of its own, quite different from the hysterical type. The latter, as has just been described, is wide and symmetrical on the two sides of the trunk as the patient faces the observer, while the former is peculiarly unequal. The inequality extends from the crown of the head to the sole of the foot, and is evidently due to a contracted Aura on one side rather than to an augmentation on the other. The narrowing is not simple, but is accompanied by a change of texture. It is singular, and it may only be a coincidence, that in all the cases (ten in number) we have seen the diminution has been on the left side. However, further investigation may show that this contraction may occur on the right, instead of the left, side. It has been found that patients—other than epileptics— have Auras simulating the shape of the typical epileptic. These will be considered later on, but they do not in the least detract from the diagnostic value of the Aura in doubtful cases.

When the Aura of an epileptic is inspected, whether the patient has had an attack lately or not, the first thing that attracts the attention is the marked increase in width on one side.[1] It will be usually noticed that the Aura on the right side of the head is one or two inches broader than the breadth of the shoulder, while

---

[1] The inequality will be found to be more conspicuous in women than in men.

on the left it will not exceed the breadth of the shoulder, and may even be one or two inches less. All down the trunk and limbs it is narrower on the left side. A detailed examination will show that the Inner Aura is equally affected with the Outer, being narrower on the left side, and this is more markedly the case round the head. Besides, it will be seen to be more opaque than normal, and striation (if not lost altogether) is very difficult to detect. The Outer Aura does not appear greatly altered except in size. When the patient stands sideways, the Aura at the back and the front of the body shows no signs of abnormality, and in this respect differs from the hysterical Aura, which is unduly wide in the lumbar region. The colour is usually grey, but occasionally there is a bluish tinge. The patients we have seen vary from twelve to forty-five years, being four males and six females.

CASE 15, Fig. 16.—X. X., a bootmaker twenty-three years old. He is a dull looking young man and has been an epileptic since he was twelve years old. During the last few years he has not had many fits. His family history is

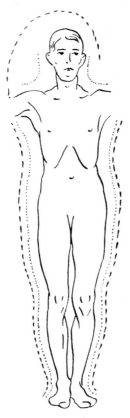

FIG. 16.—Epileptic Aura of a man. Both
Inner and Outer Auras narrower on the
left than on the right side.

extremely unfavorable. His father and mother are first cousins. The former is very neurotic (see Case 18) and becomes depressed, without any sufficient cause, for days and weeks together. His mother is a strong, healthy woman of a very phlegmatic temperament. His eldest brother has fits, but only occasionally for the last few years; is married and has four children. His eldest sister is married and childless, but seems strong and healthy, showing no signs of being neurotic. It is interesting to notice in this instance that her Aura is perfectly symmetrical on the two sides, but is below the average in width. His youngest sister is an epileptic (see next case).

The patient was inspected in November, 1909, having had only one fit during the previous two years. As he stood facing the observer the Etheric Double was plainly visible, being about one-eighth of an inch wide. Around his head the Outer Aura was about six inches broad on the right, and only three on the left. The Inner Aura was three and two inches wide on the respective sides. By the side of the trunk the Outer Aura was three and a half inches in breadth, narrowing to two and a half by the thighs and legs. The Inner Aura was two and a half inches wide by the trunk, contracting to two lower down. On the left side of the trunk the Outer Aura was two and a half inches in breadth, lessening to two by the thigh and leg. The Inner Aura was two inches by the trunk and one and a half lower down. When he stood sideways, the Outer Aura in front was two and a half inches, and the Inner two all the way down. At the back the Outer Aura was three and a half and the Inner two inches. The two Auras were less differentiated than usual. Striæ could be made out on the right side, but not on the left. The aura was, on the whole, coarse grained, especially the Inner on the left side. The blue C. C. band was even on the body, but its right extension by the side of the head was darker than the one on the left, which is exceptional. The extensions by the side of the trunk had their shades of colours reversed.

CASE 16, Fig. 17.—B. X., a girl, eighteen years of age, sister of the patient in the last case, a dressmaker, fat, anæmic, and dull looking. In October, 1908, against her mother's

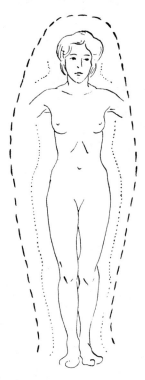

FIG. 17.—Epileptic Aura of a woman.

wishes and without her knowledge, she commenced working a sewing-machine, with the result that she fainted several times. Her own account was that she first turned hot and then cold for about five minutes, and then lost consciousness. If she went into the open air at the commencement of the attack, this would sometimes be warded off. She seemed very vague about the subject, and no further history could be obtained.

She was inspected in November, 1908, and her Aura was found to be typically epileptic; but the details are omitted as we were at that period unable to separate the Outer from the Inner Aura. The diagnosis made at the time was, that she was an epileptic. A few days later this was confirmed as she had a fit during tea at a friend's house. For some three months after this attack she had a large number of both "Haut" and "Petit Mal." As she improved, the attacks took another form, many being of a distinctly hysterical type, accompanied by screaming, and shaking of the limbs, which were to a great extent under control. Subsequently she had regularly every day a fit about an hour after getting up, and frequently a second attack during the evening. For some time she attended one of the Hospitals for Nervous Diseases, but did not gain any benefit.

On November 23, 1909, we prescribed $\frac{1}{100}$ grain of Hyoscyamine Sulphate every morning. This acted beneficially as, until January 30, 1910, she has had only two fits. One was a slight one on November 27th, when she was awakened by some curtains in her room being on fire. The fit took place immediately. And the second was on Christmas Day after the festivities. The drug was stopped at the end of December. In the middle of this month she was examined. Her Aura was well marked, grey in colour, with no rays.

Through a dark carmine screen her Aura was plainly differentiated. It was more coarsely granulated on the left side than on the right. As she stood facing the observer, no striation could be seen in the Inner Aura on the left side, and only very faint lineation on the right. The width was three inches down the right side and only two on the left. By the right side of her head the Aura was seven and a half inches in breadth, against five and a half on the left. When she raised her arms the Outer Aura was nine inches wide on the right by the side of the trunk, gradually diminishing to four down the lower limbs. On the left it was seven inches wide by the trunk, lessening to three lower down. When she turned sideways, the Outer Aura in front was three inches in breadth, and the inner two. At the back the widest extent was six inches for the Outer, and for the Inner three. The C. C. bands, both blue and yellow, were even all over the body, but the left extension of the band beyond the body was much darker than the right.

CASE 17, Figs. 18 and 19.—X. T., a schoolboy, thirteen years of age. A friend told us that the boy had "dreamy attacks" and asked his father to bring him for examination. He came in January, 1910, and purposely no questions were asked before inspection. The Aura was distinctly epileptic. The colour was a greenish grey, and, as he stood facing the observer, the Outer Aura was six inches wide and the Inner three on the right side of the head, while, on the left, it was four and two respectively.

When he put his hands to the back of his neck the Outer on the right side of his trunk was four inches in breadth, narrowing about half an inch lower down; and the Inner Aura was about half an inch less than the Outer.

On the left side the Outer Aura was only three inches wide and the Inner not quite two and a half by the trunk, and by the lower limbs half an inch less. When he turned sideways, down the whole of the front the Inner Aura was about two and a half inches wide, and the Outer a little more. At the back the Inner Aura was similar, but the Outer bulged out about six inches at the small of the back, the remainder being only three inches wide.

It is worth noticing that this protuberance of the Aura at the back is extremely rare in males. The blue C. C. band showed an even colour all over the body, but its extension on the right of the head was lighter than on the left. Strange to say there was admixture of brown in the C. C. band beyond the body, especially on the left side. The extensions of the C. C. band by the side of the trunk were very similar, except that the brown colour was not so well marked. Sub-

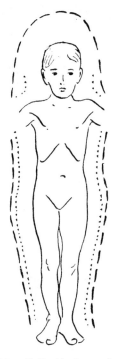

Fig. 18.—Epileptic Aura of a boy.

Fig. 19.—Epileptic Aura of a boy standing
sideways.   Unusual bulge at
back for a male.

sequently his father said the boy was under treatment for "Petit Mal" and that he had never had a grave attack.

The Auras of the other epileptics are so similar in their essential points that nothing is to be gained by describing them in detail. It may be worth mentioning, however, that all the Auras were grey, and, with one or two, there was a very faint blue tinge. In none of the cases has the C. C. band showed any change that can be typical of the complaint.

In only one instance has a patient, who is said never to have had a fit, been found to have two Auras on the one side of the body less than on the other. Personally we considered him to be epileptic, even before we could perceive the Aura, and we still hold to that opinion.

CASE 18. —I. X., a bootmaker by trade, fifty-eight years of age, the father of the patients mentioned in Cases 15 and 16. His father and uncle were both confined in an asylum, the latter until the day of his death. The patient is always dreading the same fate. He becomes suddenly and without any reason very depressed. These attacks of depression last some hours or days, or occasionally weeks at a time. They do not however prevent him from following his trade. Also, he is liable to nervous attacks, trembling, dread, etc. His Aura was inspected March, 1910. The colour was grey, and it was coarse in texture, especially the Inner Aura on the left side. As he stood facing the observer, the Outer Aura around his head was seven inches wide and the Inner two and a half on the right side, while on the left they were five and two inches respectively. By the left side of the trunk the Outer Aura was two and a half, and the Inner two inches wide. Before we inspected him, we had not the slightest idea what shape the Aura would take, but after observation, we think we may conclude that some of the attacks must have been masked epilepsy.

Diminution of the whole of the Outer Aura on one side is not confined to epileptics alone, but in no non-epileptic case has there been found a contracted Inner Aura, if the above very doubtful case be excepted.

CASE 19.—This is a very interesting case. N. D., in April, 1907, when she was twenty-two years old, overworked herself at a school, teaching all day and studying for an examination at the same time. She had very little sleep, as she was not in bed until the small hours and was obliged to get up early. She went home for the Easter holidays not feeling well, and two days after developed a high temperature, the commencement of an attack of meningitis which affected both sides of her brain. She was so ill that the nurse thought she had passed away; however, she recovered bodily, but was for two years a changed person mentally. Instead of having been unselfish, rather studious, and amenable to reason, she became perverse, selfish, and unable to concentrate her thoughts.

It may be interesting to note that Kernig's sign was well marked during her illness, remaining to a slight extent for a year and a half, but six months later could not be detected. In September, 1908, her Aura was examined. This was bluish in colour, well marked, and, as she stood facing the observer, was much wider on the left than on the right side. The blue C. C. band was even all over the body, but the right extensions were much darker than the left.

June, 1909. Her bodily health was good and her mental powers had much improved.

She has given up teaching, doing household work instead. She reads a fair amount, but not heavy books. November, 1909, she was examined again. The same character of Aura was retained, but the inequality had lessened. The Etheric Double was plainly visible on both sides being a little over one-eighth of an inch in width. As she stood facing the observer, the Outer Aura around her head was five inches wide on the right, against seven on the left. By the sides of the trunk the Outer Aura was seven inches on the right and eight on the left. By the thighs and legs there was very little difference, the extent being about four inches. The Inner Aura was about three inches wide and equal on the two sides. When she turned sideways there was a breadth of about three and a half inches in front, and four and a half at the back, while the Inner Aura was nearly two and a half inches back and front. The important point to notice is, that the Inner Aura was *equal on the two sides*. Whether this would have been the case shortly after her illness, must of course remain uncertain. This case illustrates the fact that the Aura can become contracted over a large space from a severe temporary illness, and that reparation may occur. Here is an instance of recovery both in mind and Aura, the former preceding the latter.

CASE 20.—B. T., a spinster, thirty-seven years of age, is another example of inequality of the Outer Aura on the two sides, while the Inner remained unaltered. She is in good bodily health, with the exception of a little eczema on the face. Lately she has become strange, extremely extravagant, ordering goods from the shops beyond her mother's means. At the same time her mind has never been sufficiently unhinged to justify her being placed under restraint, although she has become a very great trial to her relatives. In September, 1908, her Aura was first inspected, and showed that it was two inches narrower on the left side than it was on the right. As it was one of our earliest cases we were not able to distinguish the Inner from the Outer Aura. In November, 1909, she was examined a second time. Her mental powers remained exactly the same. The Inner Aura, as far as could be ascertained, was even all over the body, being about two and a half inches wide. While she stood facing the observer the Aura was about ten inches wide on the right side of the head and trunk, and not more than eight on the left. It narrowed gradually to about five inches by the lower limbs, being here symmetrical on the two sides. The distal margin of the Outer Aura was about three inches in breadth at the front and seven at the back. The blue C. C. band was dull across the epigastrium, being more ultramarine than blue. The right extension of the band was lighter than the left.

Case 21, Figs. 20 and 21.—N. U., a lady thirty-four years of age, who has never been robust but has never suffered from any severe illness. She has lately passed through a very trying time, which has affected her health making her depressed and thoroughly run down. She complains of pains in her head on the left side, and in her shoulders and thorax. Upon examination, the great occipital nerve was found to be very tender, and there was also tenderness by the left side of the spine, as far down as the lowest

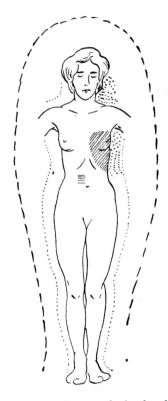

FIG. 20.—Granular Aura by head and trunk
of a woman. Light coloured patch over
the left breast and lower part of thorax.
A small darker spot near umbilicus.

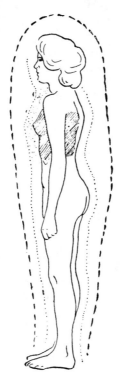

FIG. 21.—Granular Aura by head and trunk
of a woman when standing sideways.

dorsal vertebra. This was especially marked where the nerves emerge, and also in the usual corresponding spots on the thorax and abdomen. She was inspected in June, 1908. When she faced the observer it was noticeable that her Aura was much wider on the right side than it was on the left, there being nearly three inches difference by the trunk, but this was not so great by the side of the head. When she turned sideways the Aura showed no variation from what might be expected in health. The blue C. C. band had a much lighter shade over the left side of the thorax than the right. The line of demarcation was the median line of the body, but the change from one side to the other was gradual. The yellow C. C. band was correspondingly modified. In front of the abdomen the tint was even all over. When the back was examined the left side was lighter than the right, the spines of the vertebræ being the line of demarcation. In November, 1909, she was inspected again, as she was in fair health. As she stood facing the observer it was found that her Inner Aura was about three inches wider by the side of the head and trunk, and everywhere else it was only a little more than two inches. The Outer Aura was even on both sides, being eleven inches round her head, ten by the sides of her trunk, and five by her legs. When she turned sideways the Outer Aura in front of the body was five inches wide, at the small of the back seven, and lower down the limbs four inches. Although the Outer Aura was equal in width on the two sides, yet it exhibited a curious difference inasmuch as the exterior margin of the right was more sharply defined than the left, giving at first sight the impression of narrowing. This condition will be referred to later on.

In addition to the alteration in the shape other changes could be distinguished. The Inner Aura by the side of the head and the thorax as far down as the lowest ribs, was granular (fine) and not so transparent as on the right side. Below this level there was no difference on the two sides. The blue C. C. band showed a large patch in front on the left, having a lighter shade than on the right. This included the whole of the mamma and the thorax below. The lines of demarcation were distinct and sharp, the upper being the edge of the mamma, the inner the median line of the sternum, and the lower ran parallel with costal cartilages, only being about half an inch above their lower edge. On the abdomen the band was even, except for a dark patch over the right hypochondrium, lying a little above the level of the umbilicus. She complained of pain at that spot, but it was entirely superficial. On the back the band was even in colour all over, with the exception of the two small spots, one lighter in shade than the rest of the band, situated just below the spine of the scapula, and the other darker over the sacrum. The former place was tender to the touch. Quite unexpectedly the extensions of the C. C. band were even in shade.

A most important question here arises as to whether healthy persons can have their Auras unequal on the two sides? Or perhaps it would be preferable to ask "If the Aura be unsymmetrical can the person, although apparently in good health, be so in reality, or is there some local mischief or constitutional taint at work?" Unfortunately, we are not in a position to answer this question, as we have not sufficient data for arriving at a definite conclusion, because so far only two cases which could come under this heading have been seen. A careful search has been made for others, consequently we think this peculiarity must be very rare. It must be borne in mind that a slight difference in the size of the Aura on the two sides is very difficult to distinguish in males and young girls before puberty, and the detection is not made easier should, as sometimes occurs, the outline of the Aura be less distinct on the one side than the other. Accordingly we are almost restricted to observation upon women for this investigation. In each of the two examples given, the patient had certainly average, if not greater abilities than usual. In neither was there any bodily defect to cause the inequality, as both were well made and properly proportioned women. The health of each had been good all their lives, as they had escaped almost entirely the common ailments. In one of them the Aura on the diminished side did not show so sharply a defined margin as on the side on which it was normal, but having made every possible allowance for this effect, there was not the slightest doubt about the irregularity. To sum up, in these two instances the symmetry of the Aura is without any significance.

CASE 22.—K. N., a tall, healthy woman, twenty-nine years of age, whose only serious illness was ulcer of the stomach a few years ago. She was inspected September, 1908. As she stood facing the observer her Aura was seen as a light blue mist, broad by the side of her head and also by the side of her trunk, coming down to the middle of her thighs before it wholly contracted, and then it followed the outline of the body. For some unaccountable reason it was much wider on the right side, being about twelve inches at the broadest part and three in the narrowest place. On the left side it did not exceed nine inches in the widest part. As she stood sideways, it was nearly five inches wide in front of the body, and about three down the limbs. At the back it came down broad to the middle of the thighs, before it commenced to contract.

CASE 23.—E. E., a young lady nearly twenty years of age, in good health with the exception of a small cystic tumour of the left breast.

She is strong and never had any illness. Her family history is, however, by no means faultless. Her eldest sister is slightly neurotic, the third one has had three fits, and her brother's intellect is below the average. In December, 1909, she was inspected, and as she stood facing the observer, the Outer Aura was perceived to extend ten inches on the right side of the head and trunk, while on the left it was quite one inch less in breadth. Down the thighs and legs it was four inches wide on the right, and three and a half on the left side. When she turned sideways the Aura was four inches wide in front of the trunk, six at the small of the back, and down the lower limbs about four inches. The Inner Aura was three inches all over the body, but striation could not be readily seen. When she turned half sideways to the left, the position of the tumour was apparent on account of the Inner Aura being more dense and more granular over it. At the same time it looked like a small ray, being streaked, but not proceeding further than the margin. When the blue C. C. band was employed, the colour was even all over the body, except where the tumour was, where it showed a light spot. Also it was slightly darker above the pubes, owing to the advent of the menstrual period. The yellow C. C. band showed a dark patch just over the tumour.

After the consideration of the asymmetry of the whole or of the greater portion of the Auras on the two sides, the next point to be discussed is the one as to the modification of the Auras when purely local. In five cases there was a diminution, but in no case was there any sign of augmentation. Unfortunately four of these patients were seen before the separation of the Outer from the Inner Aura could be detected. However, some of the phenomena can be explained by our later knowledge.

CASE 24, Fig. 22.—H. H., a boy, ten years old, had been suffering from herpes zoster for five or six days before we had an opportunity of inspecting him. The part affected was the right lumbar region in front of the abdomen with a few spots upon the flank. The rash had reached the stage of desiccation. His Aura was plainly marked, being, as he faced the observer, six inches round the head, and two and a half by

Fig. 22.—Aura of a boy, with a conical gap on the right side.

the side of the body. It was quite normal for a boy of his age, with the exception of a portion on the right side from the level of the sterno-xiphoid plane to the crest of the ilium. From the upper level just mentioned the Aura curved inwards, reaching the body at the level of the twelfth rib. From here it commenced curving outwards, regaining its full width at the crest of the ilium. This gave the appearance of a funnel-shaped space devoid of any Aura. The point of this space seemed to touch the body, and the adjacent parts of the Aura did not appear in any way affected either in texture or in colour. Upon examination with the blue C. C. band, used transversely, the right half of the body was seen to be darker than the left; in addition the left extension was correspondingly lighter than the right. When the C. C. band was employed upon the back, the colour was normal above the eleventh dorsal spine, but below had a darker shade, the transition between the two being abrupt. All traces of the void space vanished if the boy stood in any position except facing the observer. When he turned sideways, the Aura was seen to be perfectly normal both at the back and the front of his body.

CASE 25.—Ten days after inspecting the last case we were fortunately able to examine another case of herpes zoster through the kindness of Dr. Merrick. This, too, was a boy of the same age, but the rash was in an earlier stage, having made its appearance three days previously. The rash was mainly on the lower part of the thorax in front. While he stood facing the observer the whole of the Aura on the left side of the body was quite normal, being about two inches wide, and round his head about six inches wide. On the right side the Aura, a little below the axilla, commenced curving inwards, until at the level of the sixth rib the edge apparently came into contact with the body. A short distance above the crest of the ilium the Aura began to curve inwards and upwards, until the margin seemed to touch the body half an inch below the upper curve, leaving a space without any Aura. Before investigation could be completed, two false rays suddenly appeared at the borders of the curves, one on the upper and another on the lower. These blurred the margins of the curves as they were brighter and coarser than the surrounding Aura. Directly the boy turned sideways no vestige of the abnormal space could be perceived. When the blue C. C. band was used transversely the right extension was seen to have a darker shade than the left.

Nothing more could be observed, as the boy's mother was in a hurry, having some other appointment.

In this case the brighter and denser false rays by the margins of the fissure were evidently similar to the granular appearances often seen in an Inner Aura, and most likely did not extend beyond it. Plainly there was an interruption of this Aura, and it is extremely probable that the Outer Aura was similarly affected.

CASE 26.—This is an extremely interesting case of a little girl, N. H., seven years of age, who in May, 1908, complained of a pain in the right hip, which was diagnosed as a very early stage of tubercular hip disease. Calmett's tuberculo-ophthalmic test gave a decided reaction.

As soon as possible she was sent to a Children's hospital where she remained as an in-patient until January, 1909, and after dismissal was sent to a convalescent home. In the following February, within a day or two of her arrival home we saw her. She was looking exceedingly well, had no pain and had complete movement of her hip-joint. Her Aura was fairly developed, of a greyish-blue colour, about two inches wide. It was seen all over the body as might be expected, as in any other girl of her age, except that when she stood facing the observer, there was a complete gap two inches in length in her Aura by the right trochanter major. This was so plainly visible and well marked, that her mother noticed it immediately. Instead of the edges of the Aura curving in, as in the last two cases, they were quite straight, as if a piece of the Aura had been sawn out. This space could only be seen as she stood facing, and was perfectly invisible when she turned sideways. The blue C. C. band was even all over the body, but if she stood sideways there was a light patch over the empty space. Unfortunately her family have removed to Scotland so that it has been impossible to inspect her again.

Another very interesting case has just been seen, in which there was a peculiar change in the Aura reacting under a light carmine screen quite different to any thing that has before been observed.

CASE 27.—F. D., aged thirty, a single woman who has all the symptoms of ulcer of the duodenum, was inspected August, 1910. Her Aura reached about nine inches round her head and trunk, as she faced the observer, and gradually narrowed towards the knees from whence it descended downwards unaltered. The Inner Aura, two and a half inches wide, was so distinct that it could be seen without intervention of a special screen. From the sixth to the tenth costal cartilages on the left it looked coarsely granular and very distinct. This granular appearance extended over the front of her body, as could be seen when she gradually turned sideways. When standing in this position there was nothing unusual in the Auras either in the front or back. When examined with the light carmine screen B, the Inner Aura, as she stood facing, from the seventh to the ninth costal cartilages entirely disappeared, and against the black background looked like a transparent black void space with the upper and lower margins granular; but the Outer Aura seemed unaltered, having its proximal edge sharp and the same distance from the body as the distal margin of the Inner Aura above and below. With the dark carmine screen A, the whole of the Outer Aura was obscured, leaving a gap in the Inner.

The C. C. band showed on the back a narrow strip of lighter tint than on the rest of the band by the left side of the spine about the level of the third dorsal vertebræ. In front there was a small dark patch over the central point, which extended a little more to the right side than to the left. There was a darker shade of the band on the median line of the body to the right, but the colours graduated into each other so slowly that no boundaries could be determined. This case almost proves the fact that the two Auras have their origin from different forces.

We have in the above cases instances of spaces devoid of any Aura. The space can only be seen under favourable conditions and in sections. Up to the present time none of the spaces have been observed save by the side of the trunk. The reason of this is very evident, the Aura is not so deep as either at the back or front of the body when the patient is standing sideways. The thickness of the Aura either in the front or behind, or both, will hide all traces of these vacant spaces apart from any alterations in the density. In like manner increase of density or opacity of the Aura will cause the spaces to be invisible. A suitable background is one condition absolutely necessary for their perception, and the background *par excellence* for this purpose is a dead black one; light coloured ones are absolutely useless. Taking all things into consideration for every one of these spaces seen, it is extremely likely that a number exist which are invisible.

In Chapter III it was shown that the Auric forces proceed from the body in direct lines at right angles. If from any cause a circumscribed area be deranged in some manner so that no Auric force emanates from it, while all round this affected area the healthy part is emitting Auric force in the ordinary manner, there will be formed a cylindrical void space with its long axis at right angles to the body. Instead of the deranged area, being separated from the healthy portion of the body by a sharp line of demarcation, very frequently there will be found a zone more or less affected increasing in intensity as they are farther from the diseased spot, i.e., from zero, until they have attained their natural intensity. The result of this condition will be the formation of a space conical in shape, and less void as the space expands. This peculiar formation causes the space to be much more difficult of perception, unless it has a large area, as in Case 25. The effects upon the C. C. band have already been described.

In connection with these instances another example (Case 28) has lately been inspected, which is most interesting and up to the present unique. It is a case of herpes zoster in which so large a surface was affected, that it became extremely improbable that the Aura would be wholly absent from the area of the rash. We were prepared to find something abnormal, but what shape or form the abnormal would take we were quite unable to surmise. Unfortunately the patient's Aura was not well marked, hardly up to the average in size, although easily seen.

When he extended his arm, the Aura adjacent to the rash presented a most remarkable appearance, for it looked honeycombed with vacuoles below the arm and beside the trunk. At first this phenomenon was hard to explain, but the difficulty vanished when it was remembered that the lines of Auric forces are at right angles to the body, and that in this instance some of them would come from the trunk, others from the arm, and others again from the axilla, all at different angles so that they would be continually intersecting in the vacuum, thus giving rise to the appearance of cells. This effect would also be increased by a more or less healthy Aura, both in front and at the back of the pathological portion.

CASE 28.—F. F., twenty-two years of age. A shoemaker. When a boy of about seven years of age, had hip disease, and for years suffered from abscesses caused by pieces of dead bone. He had been operated upon several times, but for the last five years has enjoyed very good health, and has had no ailment of any kind for some time until last week; he noticed a rash upon his chest followed by an eruption in the axilla, and the inner side of the upper arm; there was also another patch on his back. When examined there was a herpetic patch about one and a half inches square just below the right clavicle. The whole of the right axilla and three-quarters of the inner surface of the arm, and also another small place on the back, near the spine at the level of the third dorsal vertebræ, were covered with the rash. The blebs were very large, some being quite half an inch in length.

There could be no mistake about its being herpes zoster in a severe form.

When he was inspected it was found that his Aura was a blue grey, and below the average clearness. As he stood facing the observer on the left side it was quite normal, as the Outer Aura was three inches in breadth, and the Inner two and a half. At the front and back it showed no departure from what would be found in health, having the same breadth as just mentioned. The reason why there was no alteration seen in front of the rash, was apparently because of the healthy portion obscuring the unhealthy.

When he again faced the observer the Aura was normal around his head, but as soon as he raised his arms, the appearance just under his right arm and a little way down the trunk was very peculiar. It was granular, but not as distinctly so, as is usual when the Aura assumes this form. Against a black background it gave the appearance of a haze honeycombed with dark holes. The effect produced is most difficult to describe, and the diminution of the intensity of the granular part of the Aura seemed evidently due to the loss of substance. Besides which the Outer and Inner Auras seemed to be completely amalgamated, since not the slightest sign of differentiation could be discerned. Below this disorganized portion, the Aura seemed to have regained its proper condition for a short space. Opposite the ilium, from the level of the crest downwards, for about five inches, the Aura showed a very similar state to that described, only less well marked. This was over the formerly diseased joint.

Case 29, Fig. 23.—D., an unmarried woman

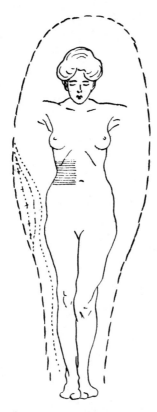

Fig. 23.—Abnormal shape of Aura with
gradual recovery.   A dark patch
on the right side.

forty-seven years of age. Her occupation is housework. She is now passing through the climacteric period. For years she has been subject to attacks of indigestion. During the last few months she has had great discomfort and frequent pain after meals, commencing about an hour and a half afterwards, and continuing for another hour and a half, or sometimes longer. There is generally a good deal of flatulency and usually constipation. The stomach is dilated.

At the end of July, 1908, she was first inspected. Her Aura on the left side proceeded from the head downwards in the ordinary manner for a woman, reaching to the middle of the thigh before it permanently contracted to its minimum. It was about seven inches broad on its widest part. On the right side it was peculiar. Around the head it was similar to the left side. When the Aura had reached the level of the nipples, being then about six and a half inches wide, it suddenly curved inwards until a little above the level of the umbilicus when it was only about one and a half inches wide. From this point downwards it continued of the same breadth. As she stood sideways there was no peculiarity of the Aura, either at the front or at the back. When the blue C. C. band was employed transversely there was a dark quadrilateral patch over the right hypochondriac region. It commenced at the median line of the body, the upper edge of which was level with the xiphoid cartilage, and the lower margin of the body. This space was several shades darker than the remainder of the C. C. band, and its lines of demarcation were sharply defined. Upon palpation, there was found tenderness of the liver, and one spot, two inches above the umbilicus and two inches to the right of the median line, was excessively tender to deep pressure. Although suspected, no malignant tumour was made out. The patient, however, improved greatly under treatment.

In October, 1908, another inspection was made. The Aura was unchanged, except on the right side. Here it did not curve in so far, and began to widen before it contracted permanently. The final narrowing occurred on the same level as it did on the left side, viz., about the middle of the thigh. Six months later the inner curvature of the Aura on the right side could still be plainly seen, but it was considerably less, otherwise there was no alteration. As the Aura appeared to be gradually returning to its natural shape, it was inspected again in October, 1909. The patient had been suffering from a return of indigestion for about six weeks, had been under treatment for three, and was much improved. The shape of the Aura, as she faced the observer, had become quite symmetrical on the two sides of the body, but the affected area was very different in appearance from any other part.

The altered portion of the Aura commenced about the level of the xiphoid cartilage, and reached to a short distance above the crest of the ilium. The Aura in this part had a dull look, was coarse in texture, and not so blue as in the healthy part, when it was examined without any screen, or through a light one. It was bounded above and below by streaks of a lighter shade, proceeding straight from the body. These differed from ordinary rays in their opacity. When seen through a dark carmine screen, the

Inner Aura was noticed all round the body two inches wide.

It was fairly lineated and the Etheric Double was well marked as a dark space one-eighth of an inch broad. In the affected area the Inner Aura was not so wide, had no striation, and was coarsely granulated. This showed that while the Aura had regained its shape, it had not assumed its proper texture. With the Blue C. C. band the quadrilateral space in the hypochondriac region was still darker than the remaining part of the band, but the difference was not pronounced. The extension of the band on the right side remained of a darker hue than did the left extension, but here, too, the colours were more even. Fig. 23 shows the gradual improvement in the shape of the Aura from time to time.

Some months later this patient was again examined, as she was in fair health. Her Aura was natural in size all over her body, and even on both sides.

However, it had not regained entirely its proper texture by the right side. Here it was coarse and opaque, but beginning to be striated, but the lines were very unlike healthy ones. The upper and lower margins of the unhealthy Aura were respectively the sterno-xiphoid plane and the crest of the ilium, and these were more plainly visible than the remainder of this portion.

With the C. C. blue band the large patch on the abdomen was still visible, but not so distinctly as formerly. It was continued round the back. Immediately the C. C. band was employed, a well-marked dark patch with undefined edges was noticed on the left side, partly on the lumbar and partly on the iliac regions. She said she had had pain the day previously in the same place, and upon palpation it was found to be tender.

Up to the present, the alterations in the shape of the Aura have been considered only when the patient stands facing the observer, thus allowing the comparison of the two sides, which ought to be equal in width and perfectly symmetrical. Whenever there is any irregularity, the Aura on the healthy side is a good standard for measurements. If, however, the patient be posed in such a manner as to permit the Aura, both in front and at the back, to be investigated, a great difficulty presents itself, as there is no natural standard of measurement for any increase or diminution in the dimensions.

Consequently allowance must be made for the great variation met with in healthy subjects, and it is necessary to depend to a large extent upon experience, and to mentally compare the Aura that is being inspected with one known to be healthy. Speaking generally, no great trouble will be experienced when dealing with Auras of males and young girls before puberty, because they are similar all over the body. With women and girls of fourteen years and upwards the case becomes more complicated, and a standard becomes essential. The best one, although it, too, is open to many objections, that we can devise, is to take some ratio having the widest part of the Aura at the side of the trunk as a unit, in which case a comparison of the breadth of the Aura, either in front or at the back of a patient with that of the side, will result in a fraction. In healthy adult women the figure for the Aura in front of the body will rarely ex-

ceed two-thirds, and in no case have we seen it
so large as one-half. The dorsal Aura, unless
the woman has a neurotic tendency, rarely
reaches to two-thirds of the pleural Aura; certainly any higher figure is pathological. In
girls having a transitional Aura the difficulty is
vastly increased, and special allowance must be
made according to the progress of the development of the Aura. So far, we have never seen
any diminution of the Aura (which can be recognized as such), either at the back or front, but
we are expecting any time to be able to observe
this modification.

Almost without exception, the Outer Aura
shows no marked increase, either of the whole
or a large portion at the back, save when the
patient is neurotic. The converse by no means
holds good, because in a fair number of subjects
who have a neurotic tendency, no enlargement
of the dorsal Aura has been discovered. There
are two main varieties of the augmentation of
the dorsal Aura, and although the division may
seem to be an artificial one, yet it represents
quite different cases.

The first variety is when the Aura comes

down from the head and is wide at the back, and does not contract fully until it reaches at least the lower half of the thighs, while in the second variety the Aura commences to increase below the shoulder, becomes broadest at the lumbar region and curves inwards abruptly a little beneath the nates. It must be fully understood that this increase is relative to the breadth of the Aura at the sides of the trunk, and the ratio is more than two-thirds. In about a dozen cases of hysteria in women and girls who have been inspected, all, without any exception, showed the peculiar shaped Aura of the second variety; and this variety seems to be almost, if not entirely, confined to this temperament, consequently it may be considered to be the special feature of the hysterical Aura.

The Auras of the first division are certainly less common than the second variety, and may occur in several distinct ailments. We have only a few examples.

1. B., a married woman, forty-two years old, who had both her ovaries removed sixteen years ago, was inspected in 1908. As she stood facing the observer, her Aura was seen to be seven and

a half inches wide at the sides, but when she turned sideways, it was also seven and a half inches at the back, and in front four inches wide. She had no neurotic tendency whatever.

2. A woman, twenty-nine years of age (casually mentioned in Case 15), who comes of a highly neurotic family, but does not herself appear to be in any way neurotic, had her Aura examined, and it was found that her costal Aura was seven inches wide, the dorsal six, and the frontal four inches.

3. An epileptic girl, who had had no fit for three years, measured at the side ten, back seven, and at the front four inches.

4. See Case 21.

5. This is a girl nearly nineteen years of age who has only menstruated twice. She is backward in development. Her Aura as she stands facing the observer is by her sides seven inches wide, and when she turns sideways, it is seen to be five and a half at the back, and in front three inches in breadth. It is probable, however, in this instance that the ratio between the different parts is merely transitory, and will become normal as she reaches the adult age.

It has been noticed that nearly every one of the patients who have an abnormally wide dorsal Aura, also have a broad frontal one.

The next step for consideration is the study of the partial enlargement of the Aura. This always occurs in pregnant women, but is only temporary, and must be regarded as purely physiological. In fact, as will be seen hereafter, the enlargement of the Aura in front of the abdomen and breasts constitutes one of the signs of pregnancy. Except in this condition, the partial increase of the Aura does not seem to be frequent, for we have only noticed one marked case. The appearance was so extraordinary that we thought there must have been some mistake, so inspection was repeated a few days afterwards with the same result.

CASE 30, Fig. 24. — A woman, fifty-eight years of age, rather stout and subject to attacks of bronchitis, but who loses all cough during the intervals, was inspected March, 1909. She had been suffering from indigestion, constipation and flatulence. No organic mischief could be found, and these symptoms vanished under treatment.

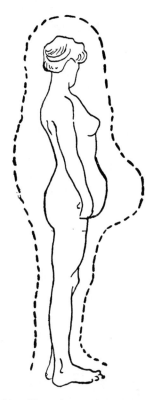

F<small>IG</small>. 24.—Very abnormal shape of Aura.

Her abdomen was very prominent and, being both fat and distended, gave her the appearance of a six months pregnancy. Her Aura was a blue grey, as she stood facing the observer; it was about seven inches wide by the sides, narrowing down to two and a half inches at the lower part of the thighs and legs. Upon her turning sideways it was seen to be at the back two and a half inches wide at the level of the shoulders, and the same width from the middle downwards, while the intermediate part bulged out about six inches. In front it was still more unusual in appearance, as in front of the thorax it was about two inches wide, increasing suddenly to six in front of the protuberant abdomen, returning about the level of the lower part of the thighs to two inches whence it continued unaltered in size down the legs. We are unable to explain this remarkable Aura.

As soon as the two Auras could be differentiated from each other we expected to find, that each of these would show at times an alteration in size and substance, and this turned out to be correct. Taking the Inner Aura first, it has been found that in the greater number of instances, in which an alteration of size has been observed, it has been accompanied by a modification of texture also, so that the two conditions will have to be considered together, and since this is the case, it will be convenient to make a few preliminary remarks concerning the change in texture that the Inner Aura is likely to undergo. It must be borne in mind that the Inner Aura, when healthy, consists of an exceedingly fine granular haze and seems to be perforated by some force giving it a striated appearance. This Aura varies very slightly in breadth by any part of the body, so that it is extremely probable that it is entirely the product of the No. 1 Auric force (page 101) emanating from the body and acting upon the ether. This force is evidently very constant in quantity and is only able to exert its energy within a short range. Its nature is unknown, but it is most likely distinct from that originating the Outer Aura.

Whenever there is any departure from health, whether general or local, this force is liable to be deranged, and consequently a modification of the Aura will take place. The disturbance always induces a change in the texture of the Aura, which can usually be perceived either with or without the intervention of a light spectauranine screen, but for the complete resolution of this alteration, it is absolutely necessary to employ a dark carmine screen. The earliest morbid change that is noticeable, is the loss of striation. Even should this not quite disappear, it will become faint and extremely difficult to detect.

Together with this want of lineation, it will be observed that the exceedingly fine granules composing the Aura in health have been replaced by others which are coarse and opaque. Apparently, each of these large granules is formed by the amalgamation of several small ones.

The sizes of these granules vary very much in different cases, but there is generally found to be a predominant number of one size which gives a distinctive aspect to the part affected. They may be conveniently classified by the terms Fine, Medium, and Coarse granules, as the case may be.

With the appearance of these granules all

structure is lost. The force which originates the Aura is usually present and remains unaltered in strength, as is shown by the breadth of the Aura remaining constant. When once the granular appearance is present, a long time may elapse before the Aura will return to its pristine state. An example may be cited of a lady who showed this peculiarity seven weeks after having a stiff neck.

Nearly five months after her neck was examined, it was again inspected. When observed in the ordinary manner there was a slight patch proceeding upwards from the lowest part of the neck. This patch at the base was about one and a half inches wide, and two in height. The distal margin consisted of a number of points one higher than the other until the highest was reached; on the other side of this peak it became lowered in the same manner. With a light red spectauranine screen the spot looked finely granulated, previously having been much coarser. When the C. C. bands were employed, the blue and the green were darker on the right side, while the yellow was even on the two sides.

As it has been found that the Inner Aura of persons in good health is usually more extensive when they are robust than when they have a delicate constitution, it is extremely unlikely when this Aura is unequal on the two sides, for the broad side to be the abnormal one.   However, there will rarely be any difficulty in determining this question, as some modification in the substance will be either seen directly, or through the medium of a C. C. band.   It will be found that, whenever there is a contraction of the Inner Aura, a corresponding change will have taken place in the Outer; but the reverse does not hold good (see Cases 20, 21).   It is worthy of notice that whenever a contracted Inner Aura has been observed the patient has been suffering from a grave malady.

Inspection of epileptics shows the Inner Aura by the whole of the left side to be narrowed, while on the right it has retained its full size, but the modifications do not cease here, as invariably on the left side the texture is coarse in appearance, or it may even be granular, while the striation can only be distinguished with difficulty, and in some instances is entirely absent. This one-sided diminution of the Inner Aura is more diagnostic of epilepsy than the narrowing of the Outer Aura which is much more conspicuous, and was first discovered. It is extremely probable that the diminution of the Aura really commences in the median line, both in the front and at the back. Nevertheless, we have found no method of verifying this supposition.

Cases, in which the Inner Aura is altered locally, are more frequent than those in which the whole or a large part of it on one side is deranged. As might be expected, some situations are more liable to be affected than others. One very common place where to find the Aura modified, is at the back over the lower lumbar regions and sacrum, slightly varying in position with different women, and presenting the usual granular appearance when seen through a dark carmine screen. When this condition occurs the invariable tale told is, that the patient suffers pain or at least a great deal of discomfort in the back during menstrual periods. As these occur at regular short intervals, there is often not sufficient time for the Aura to resume its natural state before a fresh attack of pain takes place. We had noticed long before we were able to discern the alteration of the texture, that the C. C. band very frequently gave a dark patch in this position, and we were greatly puzzled as to how it was produced. This dark patch in the C. C. band does not occur in girls before puberty, nor in women who have passed their grand climacteric, and disappears during pregnancy. As an additional proof, the young lady lately referred to never had any pain in this region during menstruation, and the C. C. band did not show the slightest change in colour. However, with her the C. C. band showed a small light coloured spot, about one and a half inches in diameter over the first lumbar spine.

When questioned whether she had any pain or tenderness in that place, she replied that there had been no pain or tenderness for the last fortnight, but previously she had had a good deal, and once the pain was so acute that she had to go to bed. This is another instance of the lengthy period taken by the Aura to become normal after being granular.

"Can the Inner Aura enlarge locally?" is a question that has been decided by observation upon pregnant women in the affirmative, and under these circumstances the change is physiological. Whether it does the same in unhealthy conditions is quite another problem, and one by no means easy of solution. In the first place when the Inner Aura has become granular as shown through the deep carmine screen, this granular portion of the Aura is often wider than the healthy. But does the granulation take place in the Inner Aura only, or does the Outer partake of the change ?

The structure of the Outer Aura must also be taken into consideration. In health the part lying just outside the Inner Aura has larger granules than the more distant parts. The different sized granules imperceptibly graduate into one another. When any local disturbance arises, those granules adjacent to the Inner Aura seem to be similarly affected but not to the same extent. As the Inner Aura becomes deranged, there is a *pari passu* alteration of the Outer, as can frequently be determined by chromatic changes shown in the C. C. band over this portion of the Aura, similar to those that occur in the Inner, it does not seem possible to decide whether there has been any increase in one of the Auras at the expense of the other. Fortunately the solution of this problem is not of any practical importance.

Case 30 is very interesting in connection with this part of the subject, because it is an instance of an evidently enlarged granular Inner Aura. The augmentation was easily measurable by comparison with the neighbouring striated portion. However, it does not throw any light upon the previous question owing to its occurrence under quite different circumstances. Here there was a primarily physiological enlargement which afterwards, on account of a local morbid action became pathologically granular.

Occasionally there is a diminution in the Auric forces accompanied by a local contraction of the Inner Aura, and under certain conditions the Auric force may cease altogether causing an absolute break in the Aura. These changes have been described elsewhere.

To sum up, the Inner Aura does not alter its

shape or size to any great extent; the chief morbid changes show themselves in alterations of the texture. It is apparent from the cases which have been quoted, that variations in shape and size of the Outer Aura are more frequent and extensive, while the structural modifications are either slight or so delicate in their nature as to be almost imperceptible.

It is impossible to say much concerning the colour of the Aura, as the preparation of the eyes for the mechanical method of perception of the Aura renders it impossible to appreciate any great variation in range of colour. The colours are for the most part limited to blue and grey, or the admixtures of the two in different proportions. Temperament and mental powers, rather than any temporary changes of bodily health, seem to be represented by the hue of the Aura. For the sake of analysis we have divided the colours into three sections. The first class contains people with blue Auras; the second those who have Auras, blue mixed with more or less grey; and lastly those who have perfectly grey Auras. The following is the result of the first hundred cases inspected. It is only right to mention that the proportion of healthy persons is much larger than our subsequent inspections have contained.

1. Blue Series.   Forty cases.

> No individual below, some above the average in mental power.

2. The Blue, with more or less grey Series. Thirty-six cases, including:

> One case of hemiplegia.
> Two epileptics.
> One case of meningitis.   Her mental powers seem to be recovered after three years.

3. Grey Series.   Seventeen cases, including :

> Two eccentric people.
> Six epileptics.
> One general paralysis.
> Three mentally dull.

Of the seven remaining patients no note was made of the colour of their Auras.

This table shows conclusively that the owners of the blue Auras are the most mentally fit.

A grey Aura seems to indicate a deficiency

of the intellectual faculty if congenital, but it remains uncertain whether the loss of brain power through disease causes the Aura to become grey, although this is probable.

It is necessary to add that, when the Aura is said to be blue, etc., there will, as a rule, be no bright colours visible, because the haze is faint and almost colourless.

CHAPTER VI

COMPLEMENTARY COLOURS IN DISEASE

THE theory of the Complementary Coloured band has already been described in another chapter. There now remains the consideration of the practical use of this band both in health and disease. Like most other scientific methods of research, a certain amount of skill is requisite. Even when the technique and manipulations have been mastered according to the instructions already given, there will remain the difficulty of understanding the meaning and the cause of any variations of the shades of the colour either on a large or a small portion of the body. It is essential to acquire RAPIDITY in the perception of the alteration of the tints, not for the sake of saving time alone, but so far as possible, to prevent inordinate strain upon the eyesight; and because the colour of the band is continually changing in shade and tint. It is during this period that the modifications are most plainly to be seen. In order to obtain a full solution of the various problems a long period of hard work and such a large number of cases are required as is far beyond our capacity and resources. The utmost we can hope to do is, to give some slight assistance to other workers on this subject.

Generally it is inadvisable, if not impossible, to examine by this method the whole of the body at a single sitting, especially if C. C. bands of several colours be employed, as the eyes of the observer become tired and incapable of appreciating slight differences in the shades of colours. For the same reason if the history of the patient be known to a certain extent, greater and earlier attention can be given to the parts of the body most likely to be affected. Again, when the shape and the general characteristics of the Aura are being investigated, an abnormality may often be detected which will point to the position of some derangement. The following remarks, unless otherwise stated, refer to the *blue* complementary coloured band as in previous chapters.

When the C. C. band is employed vertically upon the thorax and abdomen of healthy men and children, the colour will remain even throughout its whole length, unless there should be any irregularity of pigmentation in the skin. This statement neither applies to girls above the age of puberty, nor to adult women, because in this class of cases the band will have at one time the colour evenly distributed throughout, while at another it will be darker a short distance below the umbilicus. The place where this change is most prominently seen is about two or three inches above the pubes. This modification will be found to coincide with the sexual functions.

One of three things is signified by the vertical C. C. band being monochromatic on the abdomen of women. The most common cause is that the woman has finished her last menstrual period at least two or three days, and that she does not expect her next before another four or five days. If the woman reckons its commencement within this time, most probably her period will be found to be delayed. A second cause is amenorrhœa, and a third early pregnancy. At the approach of the menstrual period the C. C. band will become darkened low down, at first slightly, but increasingly as the time draws near. The colour graduates from the lighter to the darker tints imperceptibly without any definite line of demarcation, so that comparison is best made between distant parts of the band. This gradual shading is of great importance, as it often serves to distinguish between the shade of the Aura due to sexual functions, and that which is due to derangements of the abdominal organs.

Darkening of the C. C. band in the lower part of the abdomen from other causes will certainly be an insuperable impediment to the calculation of the menstrual period. If the patient be the mother of children, it will frequently be necessary to make some allowance for the pigmentation on this part of the body, but generally no great difficulty will arise from this cause, if due care has been taken. An interesting case in connection with this subject is that of a woman thirty-eight years of age, who showed an incipient darkening of the C. C. band just above the pubes. When informed that she might expect her next monthly period in about six or seven days, she replied it was not due for a fortnight. This was noted down as mistaken prognosis. However, two months later we saw the woman again. She suddenly said, "Do you remember telling me my monthly courses would take place in about a week? Well, they did seven days afterwards, being a week before the proper time." In another instance a young woman expected to menstruate in three or four days' time. With her there was no change in the C. C. band above the pubes. It eventually turned out that her period was a week later than the right date.

The knowledge gained with regard to the sexual functions by the C. C. band, when employed vertically upon the thorax and abdomen, will be a useful preliminary to other observations, because by it we can determine if there is any modification of colour in the different parts of its length, whether the change from one shade to another be gradual, or abrupt with a sharp line of demarcation; it will also show the upper and lower boundaries of the Aura in which changes have occurred. It will

be found that the band is sufficiently wide in
most cases for the observer to see whether there
is any difference in colour on the two lateral
halves of the body, and roughly to determine
their position. Subsequently the transverse
band can be used to make all the details
clear. This latter band has a great advantage
over the vertical band, for during the greater
part of the time of observation only the central
area is being used which is less difficult to see
and more free from errors of observation than
when the ends are employed. Case 21 is instructive and serves as an example. When the
C. C. band was employed vertically down the
median line of the thorax and abdomen,
the left side of the former was seen to be lighter
than the right for a considerable length, as the
higher margin of the light portion was the
upper part of the mamma, while the nether
border was the lower part of the sternum. The
vertical band showed also that the two shades
of colour were separated by a sharp line of demarcation which corresponded with the median
line of the body. Lower down the band on the
abdomen there was a small patch of a different

shade on the extreme right edge a little way above the umbilicus. This gave a useful indication for further investigation with the transverse C. C. band, the results of which have been described elsewhere.

When the observer begins to examine the spine with the C. C. band, he will find it advantageous to divide the inspection into two parts, as the band is not sufficiently long to cover the whole space from the neck to the sacrum simultaneously. It will also be advisable to notice particularly, the colour of the skin over the vertebral spines, as frequently these parts have a different hue from the adjacent portion of the body. This may be quite a natural pigmentation, or the alteration of the colour may be produced by pressure of the clothes. Directly the observer looks at the spine, he will most likely detect some alteration of the shade of the C. C. band, should there exist any abnormality. The commonest abnormalities disclosed by this band on the back, are patches on the spinal column itself, either lighter or darker, as the case may be. They may be situated upon any part throughout its length. However, the most frequent place is just over the lower vertebræ and the sacrum in women, where the band is constantly darker. The reason for this has already been stated. Two other very likely positions for alteration in colour are to be found over the last dorsal and first lumbar vertebræ, and over the seventh cervical and upper dorsal vertebræ. With the exception of the sacral patch, these are as often light as dark, and it is not unusual to find one or more patches of each variety occurring simultaneously.

Another fairly common abnormality is the appearance of a light or a dark streak by the side of the spinal column, the spine itself remaining natural.

The spots are invariably associated with pain or tenderness, not necessarily just at the time of inspection, as several weeks even may have elapsed before these pain-marks entirely vanish. The same case mentioned (on page 222) had a small light patch over the second and third lumbar vertebræ and on no other part of the body. The patient declared that she had had no pain there for a fortnight, but previously for a short time had rheumatic pain in that spot. One day it was so severe that she had to go to bed. A patch on or near the spine having a lighter tint than the rest of the C. C. band, shows conclusively that there is no organic mischief, and that the cause is temporary, and, more frequently than not, is of a nervous origin. The darker patches are generally due to a more chronic cause, besides being often the result of rheumatism. The following case is interesting as an illustration of the above remarks, also as showing an Aura of the hysterical type.

CASE 31, Figs. 25, 26, 27.—S., a married woman, twenty-eight years old, with no children, complained of sickness during the last six weeks, which was increased by any kind of worry. For three months she has been losing flesh, menses are regular, and she occasionally suffers from globus hystericus. Her thorax is peculiar in shape, being straight down, the sternal notch being level with the nipples, although her breasts are not at all pendulous. She has tenderness in the epigastrium, and pressure causes pain between the shoulders. As she stood facing the observer the Aura was ten inches wide around her head, the same width by the side of the trunk, but it suddenly curved inwards arriving at its minimum a little below the level of the pubes, from whence it proceeded downwards evenly. The outer margin was not very plainly marked. When she turned sideways, the Aura bulged out to about eight inches in width at the lumbar region, and curved inwards rapidly to a short distance below the buttocks, where it became contracted and continued downwards evenly. All down the front of the trunk and limbs it was about four inches wide. The Inner Aura was about two and a half inches broad over the body. There were faint rays proceeding upwards from each shoulder, and another ray from the lower right ribs outwards. Over the lower lumbar vertebræ and sacrum the Inner Aura was granular, and the adjacent part of the Outer was similarly affected. When the C. C. band was used over the thorax and abdomen the colour was even all over; on the back the band showed a strip of lighter colour near to and parallel with the spine, reaching from the third to the

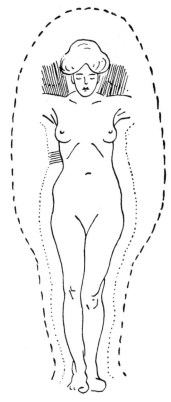

FIG. 25.—Hysterical Aura in a woman. Wide
by the trunk contracting sharply,
and narrow by the legs.

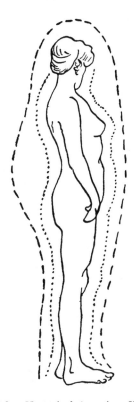

Fig. 26.—Hysterical Aura in a Woman.
Side view.   Great bulge at the
small of the back.

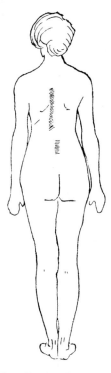

FIG. 27.—Two discolored patches on the back
seen by the aid of the C. C. band. Upper
one light, and lower dark.

ninth dorsal vertebræ. This was sharply defined in all its margins and about an inch wide, but it was dark. We considered this to be a case of nervous vomiting, and treated her accordingly with the result that she rapidly got well.

The observer must not expect to see lighter or darker spots in the C. C. band over all painful or tender places of which a patient complains. A fair proportion are invisible. Some of the discolored patches are so plainly marked that a very cursory glance will detect them, while others differ from the rest of the C. C. band so slightly that a keen sight and a trained eye are required to see them.

It is difficult to understand why some local disturbances should cause a sufficient change in the Aura to produce a chromatic alteration, while others apparently similar in every respect give negative results. Intensity of the disturbance is certainly not one of the chief factors productive of auric change. It is instructive to note that these light and dark spots in the C. C. band when projected upon the spinal column are extremely rare among males, and most nu-

merous among hysterical, nervous or excitable
girls and women.

Directly the inspection of the vertical C. C.
band has been concluded, and after having thus
ascertained as far as possible the position of any
local abnormality, the transverse band will
supplement all the information that can be
gained by this method of the use of bands. It
will have enabled the observer to examine the
two sides of the body, and at the same time to
notice whether one of its extensions has been
affected. Generally the band will be found to
be wide enough to include all the affected area,
but occasionally two observations will be required. This stage of the inspection is the one
at which to determine whether the discolored
patch is spread over the whole breadth of the
body, or only over a portion; also to determine
whether it is situated on one side of the median
line, or crosses it; or whether it is only a small
spot surrounded by the unaltered C. C. band.
When a large area is chronically affected, it
usually has a deeper hue, but exceptions are
not rare. For example see Case 21. Although
any part of the body may have a large patch of

altered C. C., yet this is met with more frequency in certain positions than in others. A common situation is the hypochondriac with half the epigastric regions. The following case is a very good illustration of the above remark.

CASE 32.—A childless woman, aged thirty, who has been married some years. She has suffered for over twelve months from pain in the stomach, which is increased after a meal and often is only relieved by vomiting. She is constantly sick, suffers from pyrosis, but never has had any hæmatemesis. The dread of pain prevents her from taking proper food, consequently she has become emaciated, weak, and anæmic.

From these and other symptoms we thought there was an ulcer of the stomach, but under treatment she gradually improved and became convalescent. When she was examined in April, 1909, it was found that her Aura was blue and there was no abnormality in shape, except that it was rather small. Around her head it was a little smaller in width than her shoulders, and as she stood facing the observer, below the arms, with her hands placed behind her head, it was eight inches wide by the side of the trunk, coming down to about the middle of the thighs before it permanently narrowed to about two and a half inches. From thence it proceeded downwards without alteration. When she turned sideways the Aura was seen to be about three inches in extent down the body and limbs. At the back it was a little over two inches wide when level with the spine of the scapula, and the same width at the most prominent part of the nates, whence it continued downwards unaltered. Between the shoulders and the buttocks there was a slight bulge extending to five inches at its widest part. Rays emanated from different parts of the body being brighter than the rest of the Aura. There were two from the shoulders, one on each side proceeding upwards by the side of the head, one from each flank going upwards and outwards, and on the right side another downwards. All these rays were visible as she stood facing us, but upon her turning sideways another ray was seen projecting from the lower lumbar vertebræ upwards and outwards.

When the C. C. band was thrown upon her

back nothing abnormal could be seen, as there were no spots of a lighter or darker shade visible. When this band was employed vertically upon the thorax and abdomen, there appeared a darker shade, commencing gradually about half way between the umbilicus and pubes. There was also another patch upon the epigastrium. As soon as this band was used transversely, it was seen that this last patch had its upper margin at the sterno-xiphoid plane, the lower about two inches above the umbilicus, and the inner border was the median line of the body, making a rectangular space from the median line to the side as far as could be seen. This was several shades darker than the remainder of the C. C. band. The extensions beyond the body, as might be expected, were dissimilar, the left being much darker than the right.

Unfortunately, after being apparently well for several months, she had in January, 1910, a relapse, and as she could not be properly attended to at home, she was sent to a hospital for treatment of ulcer of the stomach. She came out having lost all pain, and was able to eat solid food without discomfort. She was a second time inspected in March, 1910. The Outer Aura remained the same as described above, while the Inner Aura was seen to be about two inches all round her body. As she stood facing the observer, the Inner Aura was lineated on the right side, but on the left from the level of the nipples to the crest of the ilium it was coarsely granulated, and when she turned sideways the granules were seen all over the left side of the thorax and abdomen between the same levels. When the C. C. band was employed upon this part of the body transversely, the large patch could be plainly seen, but was, perhaps, not quite as marked as it had been previously. There was a slight alteration in the shape, the lower margin, from the median line curved outwards following the curve of the costal cartilages. The left extension still remained darker than the right. Two patches of altered colour were visible on the back, one by the right side of the third and fourth dorsal vertebræ. Here she had had pain, but not latterly.

The other spot was on the second and third

lumbar vertebræ. Here she always has discomfort during her menstrual periods. This
is a fairly typical case as regards the shape of
the discolored portion of the Aura. It seems
curious that the part of the Aura having an
altered tint should be rectangular, and have
the margin so straight. Several similar instances
have been seen. Occasionally, however, there is
a variation consisting either of an irregularity
of the edges, or else that the margins follow
the outline of the stomach.

It would be superfluous to enter into details
of the case of an unmarried woman twenty-nine
years of age, who was brought by Dr. Merrick,
as it is so similar to the preceding case. It
may be remarked, however, that when she was
examined by means of the C. C. band the area
that seemed to be affected was almost identical with that of the previous case; but there
was one very important difference, inasmuch as
the colour was lighter, instead of darker, than
the remainder of the band. Based upon our
former statement that the light coloured patches
were usually temporary, we gave as our opinion
that this patient's ailment was only a slight

one, and were pleased that our diagnosis turned out to be correct. A word of explanation is necessary. We had intentionally not investigated the case in the ordinary manner, as this had been done by Dr. Merrick, and it was looked upon more or less as a test case for corroboration by observation on auric changes.

Here we have two instructive cases in which the C. C. band gave diametrically opposite coloration, although the point of observation was in exactly the same part of the body. The reason for this difference is certainly difficult to ascertain, but it must be surmised that some alteration existed in the Auras of the two patients too subtle for ordinary perception, yet which was able to influence the C. C. band, and the only suggestion we can offer is that the change was a colour such as is explained in Chapter IV.

In the latter case, whatever the ailment may have been, there was in all probability a strong nervous element at work and very likely the derangement was entirely *functional*. In the former case there was chronic gastritis with its corresponding changes of tissue.

Another case interesting for comparison with these two is that of a young lady not quite twenty years of age. She was slightly anæmic, suffered from constant sickness, vomiting her food very soon after meals; also had pyrosis. She believed herself to be about a month pregnant, which unfortunately proved to be correct. When examined by the transverse C. C. band there was no alteration of colour in either the epigastric or hypochondriac regions. This indicated that a structural change of the stomach was unlikely. When the band was employed vertically, the colour on the lower part of the abdomen was unaltered. This was what might be expected either in a woman half way between her two monthly periods, or one suffering from amenorrhœa, or again one who was in the early stage of pregnancy. When her back was examined in the same way, the C. C. band used vertically was found to be uniform the whole way down. This fact will be referred to later on. As the lady was a foreigner she returned home directly she was certain of pregnancy.

Instead of the discoloration being on the left side, it may be found over the right hypochon-

drium. Here alteration in shade may be either
too light or too dark. The patch in this position
has more frequently than not, as its inner margin, the median line of the body. Its upper
edge is level with the sterno-xiphoid plane,
while its lower is about the level of the costal
plane. These boundaries are only approximate
and the variations from these are frequent.
When the discolored patch is seen in this
position, it invariably betokens tenderness of
the liver, often associated with superficial hy-
peræsthesia. Generally there is more or less
derangement of the alimentary canal beyond
the stomach, and in two cases we strongly suspected duodenal ulcer.

Another place where it is very common to
find discolorations either light or dark, more
often the latter, is in one of he groins.

Strange to say we have only seen it once in
both groins at the same time. The colour
changes may be very slight and barely visible,
or they may be considerable and easily seen.
The margins are rarely sharp in outline, and
generally shade off, very gradually into the
main colour of the band. The patches indicate

that the patient has tenderness and often pain in these regions, while the darker the hue the more intense the pain is likely to have been. It must be borne in mind, that tenderness in the groin is not always accompanied by change of colour in the C. C. band. Also, it is not common for these patches to appear without the patient having alterations in the Aura in other parts. For example we must refer our readers to Cases 34 and 13.

Instead of these large discolored areas, only small ones may be visible. In this case the patches commonly indicate that the affection causing the alteration of the tint in the Aura is entirely local, and often reveal the situation where there is pain, which may be accompanied by tenderness.

One striking instance of the accuracy of the foregoing observation is seen in the following incident. Dr. Merrick wished to see the Aura in this case and brought his patient for examination. Knowing that the patient was suffering from ulcer of the stomach, we stated that it was extremely probable that either the most painful spot or the position of the ulcer could

be detected by means of the C. C. band. No
question of any sort was asked. Dr. Merrick
was able to see the Aura quite plainly, but not
the discolored spot, as he was not accustomed to
the use of the C. C. band, and consequently was
not able to keep it on the right place, for practice is required to keep the coloured band on a
limited area.

CASE 33.—T., a married woman, thirty years
of age, has been suffering from ulcer of the
stomach for a long time. She has already been
in a hospital and was advised to re-enter, so
that she might undergo an operation, being
greatly emaciated and anæmic in consequence
of constant vomiting and hæmatemesis. Inspection showed her Aura to be well marked,
of a bluish grey colour without any admixture
of abnormality. The C. C. band, as it commenced fading, made a visible yellow spot, a
little larger than a shilling, on the left side
about two and a half inches from the median
line, a little below the level of the ensiform
cartilage. This coincided with the most tender
and painful spot, so tender a place that the
patient would hardly allow it to be touched.

The whole of the epigastrium was very sensitive, but not nearly to the same extent. Further examination could not be made.

This case presents two features worthy of notice. The first is that the spot did not merely take a different shade of the C. C. band, but completely changed its colour. Whatever its origin may have been, we look upon it as an example of a coloured ray emanating from the body (see Chapter IV). The second, that there was no large discolored area, as might have been expected. In March, 1910, she was again inspected. She had not been to a hospital as advised, but had improved greatly, having gained flesh, but still remained anæmic. She now has very little pain and only slight tenderness in the epigastrium, vomiting has ceased, although she takes ordinary solid food. There has been no return of hæmatemesis for over a year.

Still, she complains of pain in the lower part of the right hypochondrium, where also there is tenderness. As she stood facing the observer her Outer Aura extended nine inches around her head, and when her arms were upraised, the same distance by the side of the trunk, it gradually narrowed until it had reached its least width of four inches, at quite the lower part of the thighs whence it continued downwards a uniform breadth. The Inner Aura was two and a half inches wide all over the body. When examined through a dark carmine screen from about the level of the nipple, as far down as the crest of the ilium on the left side, this Aura was granular, very coarse, and, if she stood sideways, the granules could be seen occupying the same space on the thorax which looked light when the C. C. band was thrown upon it. There was besides a granular patch of the Aura on the lower part of the right hypochondrium. As soon as the patient turned sideways, it was seen that the Aura extended four inches all down the front of the body, and in the widest part at the back seven inches. The C. C. band showed a lighter patch on the left side of the thorax, commencing at the median line of the body, the upper edge being on the level of the nipples, while the lower margin followed the outline of the costal cartilages. In this light space there was an even still lighter one, exactly coinciding with the yellow spot seen at her first inspection. Also there was a small patch on the right, just where the Aura was granular.

The following is another instance of the small discolored patch being observed exactly on the place where a pain existed, on a lady who complained of pain in the right mamma. (This was found to be malignant and subsequently removed.) During the examination she said she felt a pain in the back, but did not say in what part. When she turned round the C. C. band immediately showed a light, almost circular spot about the size of a shilling over the lower angle of the scapula on the left side. It was here, and nowhere else, that the pain existed. Because this spot was light in colour, a prognosis was given to the effect that judging by the colour of this patch, the pain would not remain long. In a few days this pain quite disappeared. Nothing further will be said about the appearance of the C. C. band upon the right breast as we have not seen sufficient cases from which to draw any conclusions, and this was a complicated one.

During the consideration of the shape of the Aura in ill health, it was remarked that in cases of hysteria, the Outer Aura took a characteristic form, very different from what is found among non-neurotic people, while at the same time the Inner Aura remained unchanged. From its great constancy this peculiarly shaped Aura may be taken as a prima facie evidence of this protean malady. With the C. C. band the chief alterations disclosed are discolored areas in different parts of the body, more commonly light than dark, and transitory. Exception must be made of the three places mentioned below. In every case of hysteria examined we have found a discolored patch on one or more of the following places—the groin (usually the left), the sacrum, the spinal column near the lower dorsal vertebræ. These spots are generally darker than the main portion of the C. C. band, but are by no means diagnostic of hysteria, as they are constantly found upon other patients. The most frequent localities of the light coloured patches are in front of the abdomen and the lower part of the thorax, and at the back on any part of the spine, also near, but not touching it. If in the latter situation, they are invariably unilateral. In brief it may be said that while the C. C. band can impart a good deal of information about a case, it does not show any diagnostic mark of hysteria. Moreover, this band sometimes gives rise to no change whatever, when a predication of a marked alteration would seemingly be a certainty. The following case is a typical instance of the hysterical Aura.

CASE 34.—C., aged twenty-six, a married woman with three children. She has been delicate all her life, and before marriage was considered hysterical by her family. In August, 1909, she was thin, anæmic, very nervous and weak, and in a few days' time was to enter a convalescent home. Her Aura was well marked, being of a blue tint with a little grey. As she stood facing the observer, the Aura was about nine inches in width around her head and by the side of the trunk.

It contracted sharply a short distance below the level of the pubes and there was not more than two inches in breadth downwards. There were faint rays proceeding upwards from each

shoulder; also one slanting upwards and outwards from the left side at the waist, while on
the right side there was a light patch running
parallel with the body. When she turned sideways, the Aura in front was about two and a
half inches wide, but contracted to two down
the limbs. At the back it was two inches wide
by the shoulders, bulging out to five at the
small of the back, and then narrowing to two
at the most prominent part of the nates, from
whence it continued downwards unchanged.
There was a very distinct, but curious ray
emanating apparently from the umbilicus, proceeding upwards and outwards. This traversed
the whole of the visible Aura and was lost in
space, being at least nine inches in length.

When she was examined in front by means of
the C. C. band, the colour was even throughout
until it reached half way between the umbilicus
and pubes, where it became darker as it proceeded downwards. This deepening of the colour was due to the fact that her menstrual
period was at hand. When the band was used
transversely, there was a darker patch over the
left iliac region, commencing about an inch

from the median line of the body. No other place in front showed any colour change. The extension on the right side at the level of the waist was of the usual colour, while that on the left was darker and had a peculiar brown tinge (an impossible one to describe). There was, as might be expected, tenderness on the left side just over Poupart's ligament, and even greater tenderness on the corresponding part on the right side. This was curious, as the band did not show any corresponding abnormality.

When her back was inspected by means of the C. C. band, there were seen three distinct areas along the spinal column, having a lighter shade than the main part of the band. The upper one was over the seventh cervical vertebra, being about an inch in length, the second, about two inches long, was situated over the lower dorsal spines, while the third was over the sacrum, being about the same size. The spines of the dorsal vertebræ were tender, but not so sensitive as on either side. The sensitive part was exactly mapped out by the light patch as seen by the C. C. band. The spot on the sacrum was also tender, and the patient had constant pain there. The mark on the cervical region was by far the most interesting; as the woman said, "she had no pain or tenderness at that place," whereupon her mother immediately exclaimed: "Why, that is where you are always complaining of pain!" The answer was that "she was free from pain and tenderness at the time, and thought that was what was wanted."

This case was seen at the time when we were trying experiments for separating the Outer from the Inner Aura, and had only partially succeeded. Had we made these observations at a little later period, the light patch on the right side lying parallel with the body would most likely have been proved to be a granular state of the Inner Aura (see page 220 and other cases). It is interesting to note that while the Aura by the sides of the body was quite typical of hysteria, yet at the back and the front it was not as broad in proportion as is generally seen in that complaint. There was more blue in the colour of the Aura than might have been expected.

Why the C. C. band should show a dark

patch over the left iliac region, where the pain and tenderness were less than on the right, while over the latter position there was no change of colour, is a question impossible to solve at present. However, the following is a likely explanation. The patient had had pain and tenderness in the left groin for a much longer time than in the right, so that a perceptible change has taken place in the Aura to make it lasting, while on the right side the tenderness had not existed sufficiently long. The main objection to this supposition is that a change of shade frequently appears even when the duration of the pain has been very short. The light area seen on the neck is an example of pain from a nervous origin, making an impression on the Aura more lasting than its own duration.

The hysterical Aura occurs in women and girls who are hyper-emotional, even when they have had no serious outbreak, so that it may, in most cases, be looked upon as a product of temperament, and thus when once possessed, is extremely unlikely at any time of life to assume the type seen around ordinary women.

It is quite reasonable to suppose that the Auras of neurasthenics would assume a form closely allied in character and shape to that perceived in hysteria. However, this does not seem to be the case with any one who has had a nervous breakdown from undue strain of mind upon body, if the case has shown no previous tendency to excessive emotion. In some, and, perhaps most of these instances, the Aura will retain its natural form. The next case is a very striking illustration of this.

Sometimes, however, this affection will produce an alteration of which case 21 is a very good example, where a lady had an uneven Outer Aura with no corresponding change of the Inner, either in size or shape.

CASE 35.—C. H., a young lady twenty-five years of age. When she was between eighteen and nineteen she commenced attending an invalid relative for eighteen months, during which time she had not a single undisturbed night, although she was working hard all day. The consequence was that, upon the death of her relation, she had a nervous breakdown and, from being an unusually bright girl, she became dull. By nature she possessed an amiable disposition, but, fortunately, this part of her character did not alter. Outwardly she was a well-formed woman, but she had an undeveloped uterus, and had only menstruated three times in her life. She underwent some internal operation in the country, the nature of which could not be ascertained. All around her eyes the skin is deeply pigmented, of a dark violet hue, giving at a short distance the appearance of two black eyes. When we first saw her, she was suffering from functional hemiplegia on the right side, with almost entire loss of sensation from the clavicle downwards, and was only able to walk a few steps without the assistance of a stick. Under treatment she soon regained the use of her limbs, and sensation gradually became natural.

One peculiarity of her case was that the affected thigh was nearly two inches larger in circumference than the healthy one; the leg was also bigger, but not to the same extent. This enlargement disappeared within a few months after her recovery, when both her lower limbs were found to be symmetrical. A year later she had a slight relapse, but it did not last long. During her illness she was always desirous of getting well, and did everything she could to help, and never showed any signs of undue craving for sympathy.

In January, 1909, she seemed quite well, with the exception of a little indigestion and slight mental sluggishness. She stated, however, that she had pain in the right side of the abdomen, and the lower part of the back. When inspected, she showed an Aura much larger than the average. It was well marked, the colour being a grey blue. It extended ten inches at the widest part, and came down from over the head to the lower third of the legs before it finally contracted, being almost egg-shaped. At her ankles it was about two inches wide. There were rays, two in number, proceeding from her waist at right angles, one on either side, but they did not reach the outer limit of the Aura. When she turned sideways, the Aura in front was about two and a half inches in width, narrowing very little down the thighs and legs. At the back it was two inches by the shoulders; in the lumbar regions it was four,

and reached the lower part of the thighs before
it contracted to its full extent, being there two
inches wide. Irregular pigmentation of the
skin made the examination with the C. C. band
almost useless. Still there could be seen two
well-marked patches, one in front and one at
the back. The former was a dark spot over
the right hypochondriac region, having its upper margin level with the centre of the xiphoid
cartilage, while the lower followed the outline
of the costal cartilages. This place was tender.
The patch on the back was on the last dorsal
and the first lumbar vertebræ, which were also
tender.

Another interesting shape of the Aura remains to be considered. It is one that might
have almost been foreseen, and is characteristic
of hemiplegia. Unfortunately we have only
been able to inspect two or three cases, so
cannot say very much about them, as it is
extremely likely there may be many slight
variations. However, the following is typical
of those which have been examined.

CASE 36, Fig. 28.—B., a very tall, thin man,

fifty-six years of age, has been paralysed thirty-one years. The paralysis was a sequel to specific disease. His right arm is slightly affected, but he is able to carry on his employment as an upholsterer, though with difficulty, owing to this infirmity, which is increased by defective sight. His right leg is the limb most affected, and is smaller than the left, so that his walking power is limited. He is completely blind in one eye from neuritis, and the other is much impaired from the same cause. At the present time his general condition of health is good. He is married, and his children show no signs of hereditary taint.

He was first examined in 1908 and again in 1910. The two observations closely agreed, but in the latter the two Auras could be separated. As he stood facing the observer, the Inner Aura was the same width on the two sides, being about two and a half inches, but there was a great difference in texture, as on the left it was more distinctly lineated than on the right side of the body. At first sight it looked as if it were narrower on the latter, but that illusion arose from its being more dim. The Outer

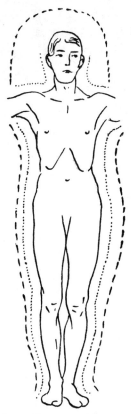

FIG. 28.—Aura of a man. Narrower on the left
side of the head and on the right side of the
body, than on the corresponding parts
of the opposite side.

Aura was most affected on the right side of the head, where it was two inches wider than the shoulder, and on the left it was four inches narrower. When he placed his hands behind his neck this Aura was barely three and a half inches broad down the right side, against four on the left. The colour of the Aura was grey. With the C. C. band the hue was even, all over the body, and the extensions, with the exception of the one by the head on the right hand side, were many shades lighter than those on the left. We have hardly ever seen such a dissimilarity of colour on the two sides. In a case like this, we think that the variation in the Aura occurs not through the influence of the motor nerves, but is due to the trophic changes usually accompanying this complaint.

Since diseases of the chest form a large proportion of cases seen in every-day practice, it might be expected that they would offer a good field for the study of the Aura. It may seem strange when we say, that chest complaints have not assisted much in our investigations of the Aura. There are several reasons for this. One very important one is that, when a patient is suffering from an acute illness, he would of necessity have to remain in bed. For obvious reasons, besides the difficulty of a background and the arrangement of light, etc., it would in most of these cases be inadvisable, if not absolutely improper, to trouble them with an investigation which of necessity must be prolonged and fatiguing, while in our present state of knowledge the benefits would be very problematical. Chronic cases, such as can be inspected with impunity, will show changes in the Aura, but none of these have any diagnostic value. Although the investigation of the Aura of these patients is very interesting, yet we have preferred to turn our attention to others, whom we thought more likely to give results which might be useful for diagnosis. The one aim of our research has been to utilise the Aura as a means of diagnosis. We shall, however, quote one or two cases which will give an idea of what changes are likely to be found. The following instance is very interesting.

CASE 37.—T., forty-three years of age, who is a married woman, complained that one day as she was getting up while coughing, she brought up some bright blood. According to her account it was quite a teaspoonful. Although a very careful examination was made, we could not detect its organic origin. Two days afterwards her Aura was inspected prior to the usual examination by auscultation, etc. The Aura had the usual shape and size for a woman of her age, and showed no abnormality until the C. C. band was employed across her chest. A light spot, about the size of a florin on the left side, in the second intercostal space and about one inch from the sternum, was immediately seen. As soon as a stethoscope was placed over this spot, fine crepitation could be heard deep down, and we believe, whether rightly or wrongly, that this was the place from which the blood exuded. Even if we had not seen this light spot on the C. C. band, we do not think we should have missed this inflamed patch, and consider that this discolored spot was due to a local inflammation, and that the C. C. band would not have shown any alteration, had it been employed two days previously, directly after the hæmoptysis. This was the only part of the lung in which we could detect any disease.

Of all the chest complaints the one *par excellence,* in which the change of the Aura might be of assistance, is incipient phthisis, but at present we have not any distinctive case to bring forward, and in fact we have been disappointed with those that were examined. Of course, in bronchitis or emphysema, where the whole of the lungs is affected, merely local alterations of the Aura cannot be expected; but should there be any change in the Aura, it will take place all over the thorax equally, and any slight variation that may be present will be too faint for distinguishing.

The following case may be taken as a typical example, and shows how little can be learned at present from the state of the Aura in chest complaints.

CASE 38.—B. L., sixty years of age. She has suffered for years from asthma and emphysema with occasional bronchitis and has had two or three attacks of cellular pneumonia. When inspected there was nothing about the shape of the Aura that was unusual. But, at the lower part of the thorax, the Inner Aura was finely granular, although coarse lineation could be seen. The left side was more affected than the right, but this was accounted for by the fact that she had quite lately been suffering from an attack of bronchitis which affected, as it always does with her, the left side more than the right.

The limitations of the Aura as a diagnostic agent are great and are increased by the want of knowledge of its origin, so that the whole of our work has been necessarily tentative, and reasoning has not helped us to forecast in what cases investigation of the Aura is likely to prove useful; nevertheless, hints may be obtained from the instances already quoted.

At present we do not know what tissues give rise to Auric forces, nor whether any or all have any control over them. One thing is absolutely certain, that the nervous system does exert a very great influence upon the Aura, and this is only what might be expected. One of the proofs of this is the power of the will upon the Aura. Already the circumstance of the prolongation or the shortening of the rays emitted from the finger-tips by merely *willing* that this should be the case, has been mentioned, and can be demonstrated at any time. Mesmerists, who naturally have strong wills and who have devoted themselves to the development of this power to modify the Aura, by means of which they can influence other people by subjecting their will powers, are further evidence that *will* can and does control the Aura.

Temperament, or the sum total of the mental and physical powers of the individual, has already been noticed as a modifier of the Aura, and it is evident that this modification is more extensive when the mental powers of the subject are great. It is not merely the area of the Aura that is affected, but also its substance, as is illustrated by the Aura of dull people having more grey in its colour, with, at the same time, a corresponding coarseness. The alterations produced by the *will* and temperament are entirely physiological effects.

As will and mind are high attributes of the brain, and are able to influence the Aura as a whole, it may certainly be expected that any derangement of the organ will modify the Aura in some way or another. Most likely a modification of the whole Aura takes place, but the changes are so refined in their nature as to be imperceptible to our senses; nevertheless, the more crude changes are capable of detection. The crude changes that are visible may be so strange that not even the most imaginative person could be likely to foresee them. For example, who could have conceived the hysterical Aura? And the more we contemplate, the more incomprehensible it seems. Among women the ovoid shape (Fig. 11) of the Outer Aura is evidently the highest form, and the more the Aura approximates to this shape the more perfect it is. The main peculiarity of the hysterical Aura lies in its being disproportionately wide by the sides of the trunk and in the lumbar regions at the back, and to the breadth down the thighs and legs. This Aura is, to use a botanical term, "Spatulate" when seen with the patient facing the observer.

We cannot tell how this shape has arisen, but surmise that there may have been arrested development below the trunk retaining the infantile form, because that type, together with the adult female Aura around the head and body, will give the peculiar shape seen in hysteria. A further confirmation of this view is, the fact that the Aura bulges out at the lumbar regions, yet contracts at the same level as at the sides.

It is useless in our present state of knowledge to speculate why this peculiar configuration occurs in women who are hysterical. The only other practical question to be solved is whether the Aura, if it have a normal shape, can change to the above type? Personally we think it extremely unlikely, as we have never seen any case in a transitional state, nor one that would lead us to suppose that such a change might take place. One curious point is, that in cases where this form of Aura occurs, there has never as yet been seen any variation in shape or size of the Inner Aura, although there are often local changes of substance, perhaps in greater variety of situations than in any other single disease. In epilepsy quite a different alteration of the Aura is encountered.

Here, instead of the Outer being only or certainly the most affected (as in hysteria), both the Outer and Inner Auras will be seen correspondingly modified, as they become diminished unilaterally, to a much greater extent by the side of the head than lower down. We cannot give any explanation why this diminution should take place, and are still more at fault why the left side is usually the one to be affected. We asked patients' friends whether during the attack one side was more affected than the other, or whether the head was turned to one side. If the convulsions were more severe on one side than the other, some light might be thrown upon the question. These questions did not produce any satisfactory answers, as, with one exception, all said they were too upset at the time to notice these symptoms. The mother of one girl said the child always showed more spasm on the right side.

We saw one of the patients in a fit, but neither side was more convulsed than the other, so that no assistance has been derived from this mode of inquiry.

When these alterations of the Aura are considered, they seem to confirm our previous suggestion that the *Forces originating the Outer and the Inner Auras are distinct,* as the latter never seems to be deranged over a large space, without some variation of the former taking place; on the other hand the Outer may be altered while the Inner remains unchanged.

There is not the slightest doubt that the Aura is affected locally when there is some local disorder of the nerves, but whether the alteration is the direct outcome of the nerve disturbance (similarly to a functional derangement of an organ), or whether it is the affected organ that produces the change in the Aura, is at present uncertain. Most probably either may be the cause, and in many instances the two are jointly concerned. One fact stands out prominently, viz., that a local disturbance influences the Inner Aura with much greater frequency than it does the Outer, and when the latter is affected the former rarely escapes derangement. (Cases 23, 24, 25, are instances in which the outer Aura has become locally altered.) This is the reverse of what usually occurs when the whole or the greater part of the side is affected.

A case of neuralgia may be taken as an example of the manner in which the nervous system primarily operates upon this Aura. Case 21 is a very good example. When seen late in 1909 it was noticed that the whole of the Inner Aura adjacent to the painful parts was altered, as it had lost all striation and had become coarsely granular in appearance. The Outer, too, showed signs of derangement, as the distal portion was less plainly seen than is usual, giving it the aspect of having lost part of its substance, as it might be otherwise stated, No. 2 Auric force was not so great as if healthy, but at the same time there was no alteration in its general character. If the force had been still less the Aura would have been seen smaller than normal. This was the condition of the Aura when first seen in 1908, and it is evident that in 1909 it was regaining its natural conditions.

In an acute case of neuralgia, a girl, thir teen years of age, had a spot at the level and two inches to the right of the third dorsal vertebra, where she had paroxysms of pain coming on suddenly and often lasting for hours. The most common time for its accession was at night, sometimes just before she went to bed or soon after, and at either time the pain would awaken her. There was no tenderness over the place, and no cause could be found to account for it. It was very intractable to treatment for some weeks, but had improved a little when she developed appendicitis, and immediately the pain vanished and never returned. Her Aura was examined, and was found quite natural all over the body, with the exception of a small patch just over the painful spot which had become finely granular. It was only in the Inner Aura that any change could be discovered, as the patch of the Aura affected must have been very small. It would hardly be likely for the Outer Aura to show any change, since the surrounding healthy portion must have obscured any that did take place. In this instance the blue C. C. band showed a dark spot, while in the last case the affected Aura induced a lighter shade.

A man suffering from sciatica exhibited similar changes in the Aura down the whole of his thigh.

When a nervous derangement causes a local organic change of tissue, it is probable that the modification which takes place in the adjacent Aura is due partly to the nervous element and partly to the diseased tissue, but it is next to impossible to decide the proportion dependent upon each. Herpes zoster is a very good example of these combined causes, producing a marked and interesting change in the Auras, but so much has already been said about these alterations that the reader is referred to Cases 24, 25 and 28.

As these cases show that the nervous system induces alterations in the Aura, both with and without a corresponding change in the local tissues, it may perhaps be thought that the modification may be entirely owing to the influence of the nervous system, and that the altered tissue has nothing to do with causing it. The only method of disproving this hypothesis is to find some instance where there is a change in the Aura that cannot be credited to the action of the nervous system. Fortunately we have three marked instances in which it is extremely unlikely that any nervous agency can be present. All these cases are tumours of the breast, two fibro-adenoids and the other cystic.

In none was there any pain, and they were only discovered by accident. In no case could any alteration of the Outer Aura be discovered, but each deranged the Inner Aura. One fibro-adenoid caused the Inner Aura to *assume the similitude* of a small ray not more than one and a half inches in length, being about slightly more than half the width of the Inner Aura, and this ray was finely granulated. When viewed with the blue C. C. band it exhibited itself as a spot lighter than the remaining portion of the band, especially as the colour was fading. With the yellow C. C. band this patch was darker.

The second fibro-adenoid instance was almost identical. The remaining case, too, was very similar, as only the Inner Aura was affected for its whole width, and the change consisted of a coarse granular state replacing the ordinary Aura just over the tumour. When this was examined by means of the C. C. bands the blue showed a light, and the yellow a dark patch.

From the above remarks it may be taken for granted, that although the nervous system has a very great, perhaps a predominant control over the Auras, yet other tissues, when in an unhealthy state, do influence them as well. In connection with this subject it will be interesting to compare Case 33 with Case 31. In the former the patient had an ulcer of the stomach which caused the part of the C. C. band in front of it to be altered, besides causing a good space around it to be lighter in tint than the rest of the band. Also the Auras were coarsely granular in the gastric region. It must be noticed that there was no change in tint of the band near the dorsal vertebræ.

In the latter case, although the woman was suffering from constant vomiting, yet there was only a slight granular appearance of the Auras in the gastric region, and the C. C. band did not disclose any change of colour in the front of the body, but on the back there was a narrow streak lying close to the spinal column on the left side, from the third to the ninth dorsal vertebræ, which was decidedly lighter in colour than the remainder of the band and had sharply defined margins.

In the first of these cases, it looked as if the diseased organ was almost entirely the factor producing the alteration in the Auras, while in the latter the deranged stomach only affected the Auras slightly, but the main change in the band was due to the nervous system.

Although it seems fairly certain that some diseased organs do produce a change of some kind in the Auras, yet there are instances in which we have looked for it without any success. Two or three cases of granular kidney have been inspected, but in none has any alteration of the Aura been detected. One of these patients had been afflicted with this complaint for many years, and inspection took place a short time before he became hemiplegic with a fatal result. It is possible that the reason why in these cases the Auras showed no alteration is that the depth of the superincumbent healthy tissue annulled the influence of the diseased organ, together with the fact that the change in the kidney is a degeneration of a passive rather than an active type.

CHAPTER VII

THE AURA DURING PREGNANCY

It frequently occurs that a patient asks a medical man whether, after she has missed either one or two monthly periods, she is pregnant. The answer usually given "to wait a little time," is not always acceptable. The difficulties of arriving at a correct conclusion in very early pregnancy are very great, so that any fresh method that can aid in diagnosis will no doubt be appreciated. It must be understood that in the following plan not one single sign of pregnancy can be accepted alone, but when one or more point to the same direction, the probabilities are so great that the conclusion, one way or the other, is almost positive. There are three distinct signs of pregnancy associated with some change in the Aura; two are arrived at by investigation by the C. C. band, and the third is a slight alteration in the

shape of the Aura and its texture. These will
be considered seriatim.

When a woman is inspected for early pregnancy, it is advisable in the first place to ascertain whether her Aura is normal in shape
and size, not merely by the sides, but by the
front and back. In nearly every case of pregnancy which we have examined, the Outer Aura,
all down the front of the patient, has seemed to
be wider on the whole than usual, never exceeding, however, the limit given on page 16. At
present it cannot be decided whether there is
any absolute increase, or whether the enlargement is illusive and due to the tendency of the
Aura to be slightly altered in texture, and thus
made more perceptible.

Whether this be the case or no, there can
usually be observed some slight increase of the
Outer Aura at the lowest part of the abdomen,
when the patient is standing sideways to the
observer. Also, if she has not turned round
quite as much, but sufficiently to allow the
contour of the breast and nipple to be silhouetted upon the black background, it may
here, also, be seen to be a little enlarged. At

the same time in both these positions the Inner
Aura will look more dense and bright, giving
the effect at first of a granular appearance.
This is especially noticeable in front of the nipples, where it is more prominent than around
the other parts of the breast, and sometimes
forms the appearance of a small ray.

One most important fact to be remembered
is that the Inner Aura is not granular, but
remains striated. This lineation shows there
is no morbid action taking place, but that there
is only an increase of physiological action.

After the patient has had her Aura inspected
directly, it is necessary to commence the colour
test. For doing this she must face the observer
when he employs the C. C. band vertically, and
he will perceive the colour even throughout the
entire length, if she is in good health and pregnant. He ought to take special notice of the
part of the band on the lower portion of the
abdomen near the pubes. The full significance
of this test is, that the patient shows no sign
that the act of menstruation is near at hand.
When the C. C. band is employed transversely
over the breasts, the colour with women who

are not pregnant, or who are not nursing an infant and have no affection of the mammæ, is naturally even (except over the areola and nipples), not solely on the breasts themselves, but also on the adjacent parts of the body. In pregnancy and in lactation it is common to find the C. C. band over the breast to have a lighter shade. The lighter tint is due to a change in the Aura similar to that which has been considered in Chapter VI. This alteration of tint has no meaning in itself, but is a good corroboration of a change having taken place in the Aura surrounding the breasts. When the transverse C. C. band is thrown upon the epigastric and hypogastric regions, no change of colour will be shown, although the patient may be suffering from nausea and vomiting, pointing to the fact that the gastric disturbance is not so dependent upon a local derangement as upon some nervous influence.

Case 31 is an analogous instance where the stomach troubles were due to pregnancy. If the patient has previously been suffering from an affection of the stomach this statement, of course, cannot hold good. No other assistance can be obtained from the C. C. bands when employed on the front part of the body.

It has been mentioned, that in a large number of women, a patch of larger or smaller extent upon the lumbo-sacral region of the back can be seen, which causes the shade of the C. C. band to become darker than the remaining portion. This has been attributed primarily to the sexual functions, and directly to the peculiar granular state of the Aura.

Strange to say, that in no case of pregnancy have we seen the Aura to be granular, and consequently the darker patch has disappeared. We consider that the presence of this dark patch is presumptive evidence against pregnancy. Absence of it in a woman who is known to have had this discolored spot, or if she is in the habit of suffering a considerable amount of backache during her menstrual period, is a very important, if not an absolute sign of being pregnant, unless there is some known reason which is likely to remove it.

When the C. C. band is employed on the lower part of the abdomen with the patient standing sideways the colour of the extensions may be dissimilar. When this is so, the front is more likely to be lighter in shade, confirmatory of the alteration of the Aura in this part, as has been discussed above.

To sum up the signs of early pregnancy as shown by the Aura are: (1) A slight increase of the Outer Aura at the lower part of the abdomen and in front of the breasts.

The Inner Aura is increased in distinctness, but remains striated.

(2) The C. C. band shows no discoloration on the lower part of the abdomen.

No discoloration over the stomach, even if nausea is present. The band is often lighter on the breasts.

(3) Absence of the dark patch on the lumbo-sacral region.

The two following are illustrative cases:

CASE 39.—L. K., aged twenty-nine. She has been married nearly two years, and hopes she may be pregnant, as she missed one period and a second is nearly due at the present time. When inspected, as she stood facing the observer, her Outer Aura was ten inches wide round the head and trunk by the side, gradually diminishing to five at the ankles. The Inner Aura was two and a half inches in breadth all over the body. When she turned sideways to the observer, the Outer Aura at the back was four inches in breadth widening to six at the small of the back. In front, taken as a whole, it was about four inches wide all the way down, but there was a slight increase in front of the breasts and a slight bulge at the lowest part of the abdomen. In these two places the Inner Aura looked coarse and consequently more distinct, but was striated. When the C. C. band was used on this portion the extension in front was lighter than at the back. As she again faced the observer, the C. C. band when used vertically, was even all the way down the front with the exception of the small parts over the breasts. When used transversely over the breasts, these were lighter in shade than the adjacent parts. There was no alteration in the tint of the gastric region. When the back was examined the colour was unaltered in any place. The lessons to be learned from this case, are first, that the woman did not show any signs of approaching menstruation, although it was due. Next the Aura disclosed the fact that there was physiological activity going on in the breasts and in the part of the abdomen just above the pubes. There was no doubt about the case being one of pregnancy.

CASE 21 (continued from page 189).—In this instance the lady believed herself to be pregnant, having missed two monthly periods and was near her third. However, there was no alteration of the Aura round her right breast, nor any increase of the abdomen just above the pubes, neither was there any discoloration in this place when the C. C. band was employed. On the back there was a prominent dark patch as seen with the C. C. band over the sacrum. In this case the only sign of pregnancy was the absence of the discoloration of the C. C. band just over the pubes. The diagnosis was made that pregnancy was out of the question, that menstruation would not take place within four or five days, but when, could not be foretold. As a matter of fact it occurred just seven days after the inspection.

As pregnancy proceeds, the changes of the

Aura in front of the mammæ and abdomen increase, but not equally. The part adjacent to the breasts does not enlarge to an extent corresponding to that in front of the abdomen, and is variable in size. It is not only the Outer Aura which expands, but in many cases also the Inner. Even when the Inner Aura has not increased, it will have become more distinct than the neighbouring parts, showing that the gland has become ready for the assumption of its special function. Usually, it will not be difficult to determine whether this Aura in front of the breasts has enlarged, because it can be so easily compared with that of the adjacent parts either above or below. Although it may look finely granular with or without the intervention of a light screen, yet the *A* carmine screen will disclose the striated appearance of health.

When the Aura in front of the abdomen is examined after the woman has reached her fifth month of pregnancy, it will be seen to have become wider than during the earlier stages, and may continue to increase until near the birth of the child. The Auras of pregnant women after the fourth or fifth month may be divided into two classes, which, although they are not very unlike, yet have a distinction which is by no means artificial. In one group the Aura is not so much increased as in the second; besides, the shape is more regular and follows with greater exactitude the contour of the body. When the woman stands sideways to the observer, and the Auras are differentiated into the Inner and Outer by the carmine screen, the former will be seen to be slightly enlarged and to keep a proportionate width to the Outer Aura throughout.

In the second group the patients have their Auras broader and more distinct in front of the most prominent part of the abdomen, than beside the less protuberant portions, causing the Aura to be conical, and giving the impression that it is wider than it is in reality. When the two Auras are separated, the Inner, too, will be seen to have a tendency to become conical, being a little wider in front of the most prominent part of the abdomen, but not to the extent of the Outer. This is a good instance of the Inner Aura growing larger and subsequently diminishing as it regains its natural size shortly after parturition.

When the C. C. band is employed, the whole of the breast except the nipple and the areola, will usually appear lighter than the neighbouring parts of the body, whether the patient be standing facing or sideways.

The C. C. band when thrown upon the thorax or abdomen will sometimes be even and at others darker on the latter. If the woman turns sideways to the observer, and the transverse C. C. band be thrown upon the abdomen, in the second group of cases where the Aura is conical, the extreme point of the protuberant abdomen is usually lighter, and the front is lighter than the back extension. In the first group of cases the C. C. band is even throughout.

The paleness of the colour over the breasts and abdomen associated with the enlargement and definition of the Inner Aura, indicates that it is extremely probable that some change in the Aura has taken place, and is an extra proof that "a change of texture in the Aura can cause a sufficient alteration in the C. C. band to change its tint." The following case is extremely interesting: —

CASE 40.—Mrs. T., aged thirty years was pregnant for the fourth time. When inspected she had reached the sixth month. The history she gave was that she had been feeling exceedingly well the whole time, but three weeks previously she was awakened in a fright by a row in the house. From that time all movement of the child ceased, and the abdomen was getting smaller, although previous to the upset the movements of the child were uncomfortably strong. She was depressed thinking the child was dead.

Inspection of the Aura at the sides and back showed it natural in every respect. In front, as she stood sideways to the observer, the Inner Aura was about three inches broad down the thorax and lower extremities, except that it was slightly more marked in front of the nipples. Before the prominent abdomen it was about two and a half inches wide. The Outer Aura was three and a half inches down the whole of the body, except in front of the abdomen where it was conical and became about eight inches wide. The main interest was centred in the condition of the Inner Aura. This, above the

sternal notch and down the thighs and legs,
was finely striated as is usual in a healthy person.   The part before the lower third of the abdomen was distinctly granular (coarse), while in
front of the upper two-thirds it was coarsely
lineated, but the lines were not well marked.
It was in a transitional state between the granular Aura and the striated.   Thus it could be
seen that the Aura was normal all round the
body with the exception of the part in front of
the abdomen where it was pathological.   The
C. C. band showed nothing unusual, but it may
be worth stating that it was lighter on the left
breast and darker on the right, than the remaining portion of the band, and at the same
time the colours of the two extensions were
even.   The explanation of this effect happens to
be quite simple, because the tint on the left
breast is what is common during pregnancy,
while the right breast was distinctly pigmented,
and being quite healthy did not affect the Aura
beyond the body.

We think that in this case a diagnosis of a
dead child was justified.   Subsequently, when
the uterus was palpated, it was found to be more

soft than is usual at the sixth month of gestation. No signs of any uterine souffle nor fœtal heart-beats could be distinguished. Two months later she was delivered of a dead male infant.

In conclusion we know our shortcomings and only hope that our readers will overlook them, as the subject of seeing the Aura through the intervention of screens is quite a new one. So many unforeseen difficulties have arisen, and peculiarities detected from time to time that it has been necessary to commence observations *de rovo* more than once. We shall be quite satisfied that our labour has not been wasted, if science, especially as regards medical diagnosis, has been advanced one iota and we fervently hope that more competent investigators will take up the subject as there is a vast field for useful research.

Lastly we must thank our friends, some of them who have put themselves to great personal inconvenience, for their kind assistance.

APPENDIX

APPENDIX

It has already (Chapter III) been stated that the Auric stream issuing from the tips of the fingers, can be either elongated or contracted according to the will of the owner. For some time we had been intending to investigate the subject of the Will power upon the Aura, but until quite recently have had no opportunity of doing so. Several essentials are requisite for successful experiments. These are, that the patient should have a well marked Aura, both Outer and Inner,—should be in good health,—should take an intelligent interest in the subject,—should have a fairly strong will with ability to concentrate his mind,—and perseverance if not at first successful.

CASE 41.—At last a favourable opportunity occurred during the inspection of a young woman G. 2 (see Table 2 and note), just under twenty years of age who was late in development. Her case is interesting on account of the rapid increase of her Aura in eighteen months. When seen in the Spring of 1909 it was barely seven inches by the waist, and now it is quite nine inches. Menstruation has set in and she looks a picture of health When last inspected her Aura was very distinct, healthy in shape and appearance, and even in brightness all round her body, without showing any signs of rays,—in short an ideal one for our purpose. Before commencing any experiment we showed her how the Aura emanating from the tip of one finger could be extended or diminished at will, and asked her to try and influence hers in the same manner. This, she almost immediately succeeded in doing, so we requested her to endeavour to perform the same in different parts of her body, to which she agreed. The first place chosen was the crest of the ilium, as that was considered a very suitable place, because we had never seen a beam radiating from it, although theoretically it would be a likely situation for a ray, being a prominent ridge. After about half a minute from the commencement of *willing*, the Inner Aura looked brighter and gradually extended outwards and upwards as far as the margin of the Outer Aura. When the ray thus formed had reached this point, she stopped willing and the ray rapidly receded.

The next place chosen was the lowest part of the thorax, while she was standing in the same position, viz., facing the observer. It is not at all uncommon to perceive rays proceeding straight out from this situation, and also it is one of the most frequent places for rays of the first order or patches of light to appear. The result was hardly what was expected, as instead of a ray proceeding outwards, the whole of the Inner Aura from the sixth rib to the crest of the ilium became bright without any extension.

The two shoulders, first one and then the other, were the next two spots selected for the emanation of the rays. Here there did not seem to be any difficulty as the beams manifested themselves almost directly, taking an upward and outward direction.

The patient now turned sideways and began willing a ray to extend from the tip of her nose. In this she was perfectly successful, as it appeared almost immediately and stretched outwards seven or eight inches. This was beyond the external margin of the visible Outer Aura.

As she was evidently becoming tired, the experimenting was concluded by her inducing a ray to emanate from the nipple. This occurred instantly she began to will, but at the same time the whole of the Inner Aura in front of the breast became brighter.

It has already been shown that the Aura adjacent to prominences of the body is more susceptible to external influences, owing to the fact that the auric potential is greater upon points than upon plane surfaces. For the same reason it is only natural to suppose that the *will power* would be able to exert its influence more easily and powerfully upon the Aura in front of protuberances than elsewhere. The first mentioned experiments conjoined with other similar ones prove that such is the case. But, in coming to this conclusion, it must not be forgotten that the concentration of the mind upon the given spot which is to be influenced, is much more easy when this is naturally a distinct portion of the body, than when it is only a point in the midst of a large even surface.

Besides, during these experiments we have noticed that when the patient has become fatigued, the power of concentration is lessened, the effect upon the Aura is decreased in intensity, and at the same time spread over a larger area. In the above instance when a ray was willed to proceed from the nipple, it was seen that the Inner Aura surrounding the breast was similarly, although to a less extent, influenced. Had this effect been confined to a solitary case, it might have been supposed that fatigue was the cause; however, the experiment has been repeated, always with the same result, even though the patient may have been quite fresh. This phenomenon is most likely due to the intimate physiological connection between the gland and the nipple which prevents one being influenced by the mind without a corresponding change in the other.

As soon as it was certain that *will power* could produce extensions of the Inner Aura into rays, it became a natural sequence to expect that colour changes might be induced by the same means. This, if it could be done, we considered as extremely important since it affords a solution of a most difficult problem, and at the same time proves the truth of the theory previously advanced in Chapter IV, viz., that colour changes were frequently the origin of the lighter or darker patches in the C. C. bands. For this purpose we engaged an artist's model.

CASE 42.—D., a married woman, twenty-eight years of age, who has had two children, was inspected during October, 1910. At first her Aura was examined in the ordinary manner. It was distinct having a grey blue colour. As she stood facing the observer, the Outer Aura around the head and trunk was about ten inches in width, but it narrowed sharply a very short distance below the level of the pubes, when it became only four inches broad. The Inner Aura was three inches by the head and trunk, and slightly less by the sides of the lower half of the thighs and legs. When she turned sideways, the Outer Aura was seen in front to be five inches by the trunk and four lower down; at the back it was four inches by the shoulders, bulging out from that place until it became about eight inches at the waist, contracting suddenly just below the buttocks to about four inches, keeping this width down the lower extremities. The Inner Aura was three inches wide by the head and trunk, and a little less below. The C. C. band showed only one patch upon the sacrum which was a little darker than the proper tint. Otherwise the colour was even all over the body. The extensions of the band by the side of the body were alike, both as she stood with her arms upraised and also in the spaces between the trunk and arms where her hands were placed upon her hips and her elbows extended, as she stood facing the observer. She was in excellent health, but as might be surmised from the shape of the Aura had a hysterical temperament.

As she was not conversant with the process of *willing*, we thought it advisable to commence with trying to obtain rays from different parts of the body. This she accomplished without much difficulty, but as the experiments differed from those in the last case by only minor variations, they will not be quoted; however, it is worth mentioning that the first ray took the longest time to induce, while each successive one was quicker, until the last ray flashed out almost instantaneously. As she was able to see the Aura easily, she was also able to perceive the rays quite distinctly, sometimes even before the observer could. By this time she seemed "*au fait*" at willing, so she commenced endeavouring to induce colour changes of the Aura. Because it would be useless to have merely an abstract idea of a colour, and as it would require the expenditure of a considerable amount of energy to convert the abstract into a concrete idea, especially in the case of a novice at the work, she was shown a book with a red cover.

EXPERIMENT 1.—She stood facing the observer with her hands upon her hips and her elbows extended, so that there should be a space bounded entirely by the trunk and arms. She was requested to *will* the Aura in the left space to become a colour (darker portion of crimson alizarin) corresponding to the book. In about a minute she said she could see the Aura changed in hue, being a scarlet red, but could not make the same colour as the book. Afterwards she pointed out scarlet vermilion as the colour her Aura had assumed. What appeared to the observer to occur, was this. At first

there was no change in the Aura, both sides
being similar. Then some indefinite and inde-
scribable alteration took place; ultimately the
whole Aura seemed to vanish, leaving the space
black; it then reappeared and disappeared in
turns, two or three times, when the space became a grey red (grey and vermilion) instead
of being as at first a grey blue. Only the Inner
Aura was affected, and the part nearest the
axilla was decidedly more red and dense. She
was asked to keep on *willing* while the black
background was being changed for a white one,
to allow an examination with the C. C. band to
take place. The right extension of the C. C.
band remained exactly the same as when it was
seen before the experiments commenced, but on
the left side the extension was very much darker
with the blue and yellow C. C. bands, while
with the red it was at first darker, and, as the
patient became a little fatigued, it appeared
lighter. In order to eliminate any errors from
uneven illumination, she turned her back to the
observer. The blue and yellow C. C. bands
showed the left extension darker, and with the
red C. C. band it was lighter, as nearly as possi-

ble the same tint as was perceived in the first position. It is interesting to note that another observer at a different inspection, saw this vanishing and return of the Aura in the same manner as has just been described.

EXPERIMENT 2.—She was now desired to *will* the right space by the side of the trunk a blue colour, which she did with comparative ease. The colour of the blue obtained was the darkest shade of permanent blue. After raising her arms and placing her hands behind her neck, the Aura on the right side continued blue, while on the left side it still retained the red shade even down the thigh and leg. Certainly it was a weird sight, seeing a haze on one side of a person red and on the other side blue.

EXPERIMENT 3.—While still standing with her arms up, she tried to will the Aura on the left side, yellow. She said she could see plainly that colour, but to the observer the hue, although changed, never became a true yellow. The nearest colour we have to it, is the darkest shade of roman ochre. The names of these colours have been taken from the specimen sheet of colours of G. Rowney & Co. Of the colours red, yellow, and blue the latter is the easiest to will, while yellow is the most difficult.

Interesting as these experiments undoubtedly are, we consider them only preliminary to the following crucial ones, which although not so effective are more valuable. Our chief aim has been all along to obtain a coloured ray emanating from a circumscribed area, part of a large plane surface, not from any projection of the body. Besides, certain other conditions are absolutely necessary for our purpose, the first being, that the Aura surrounding the ray shall not be influenced at all, or at the most, to a very slight extent. This means that the patient must be able to concentrate the *will power* upon a very small spot. A second condition is that the ray shall proceed outwards at right angles to the body, and come straight towards the observer. In all probability this will cause the ray to be invisible in the ordinary way, owing to the fact that the skin makes a bad background. Lastly, that the patient can keep the ray unaltered for a sufficiently long time for it to be critically examined by the aid of several C. C. bands. As we were aware of all these inherent difficulties, we were agreeably surprised at the results of the first trials, which were due not a little to the painstaking efforts of the patient, who, before they were finished, was beginning to lose her *will power* from fatigue. Her power of perceiving the coloured rays was a very great help as she could inform us when to look for them.

EXPERIMENT 4.—For the first trial, a small area half on the right breast and half over the sternum was chosen, and she was asked to *will* the Aura at this place *red*. Within a minute she said she could see the spot red, while it was completely invisible to the observer. However, when looked at by means of the C. C. bands, it could be seen darker when the yellow or blue band was employed and lighter with the red band.

EXPERIMENT 5.—The next test was for her to *will* a small area not exceeding an inch in diameter, somewhere or other upon the abdomen, to become red, only she was not to tell the position of the spot. Directly she said she could perceive the place coloured, we examined the abdomen with the blue C. C. band and almost immediately detected a darker small spot, a little above and to the left of the umbilicus. We placed our finger upon it, the exact centre of the place she was willing for the Aura to become red.

EXPERIMENT 6.—She next tried *willing* the Aura over an unknown place on the thorax, choosing yellow for the colour. As soon as she said she was ready, we looked for the spot with the blue C. C. band. This showed a dark patch about two inches in diameter; not very well defined, upon the upper half of the left breast, and we placed our finger upon the centre of it. This instead of being in the middle of the place she was willing, was only on the edge of it, which would be about half an inch from the true centre. The diffuseness of the colour change was due to her being fatigued. No more experiments of this nature were possible.

INDEX

INDEX

A